Mistress of Mirth's
COMEDY TOUR

Mistress of Mirth's COMEDY TOUR

a woman at her wits end

JUSTINE SLESS

ASPASIA

First published 2022 by Aspasia
the general books imprint of
Australian Scholarly Publishing Ltd
7 Lt Lothian St Nth, North Melbourne, Vic 3051
Tel: 03 9329 6963 / enquiry@scholarly.info / www.scholarly.info

ISBN 978-1-922669-37-7

Cover design: Sarah Anderson

To my daughters Ruby and Jess.
Take Up Space. Make Some Noise. Know Your Power.

Contents

The C.O.M.E.D.Y Tour

C.O.M.E.D.Y is an acronym for Call Out Male Entitlement Daily, Y'all. The Tour begins in Bourke Street Mall, where trams trundle by, buskers busk, and throngs of people go in and out of shops.

'Welcome to the C.O.M.E.D.Y Tour, my name is Justine Sless and I am a comedy addict, my gate way drug was that first time I ever did a gig in the back of a bar, on a makeshift, dimly lit stage. It was an incongruous, hostile and seminal moment. Not least because I was attempting to illicit laughter but also trying to come to grips with how absurdly undermined I felt by the whole process of doing an unpaid gig with a blatant undercurrent antipathy.

'The Tour takes only three people as it aligns with the joke-telling rule of three. The sequence of the rule of three is: establish, reinforce, surprise.[1] Like when my kids were little I would always give them an instruction and follow it up with a weather report: 'You haven't even got your jacket on, get in the car it's freezing. You won't need a singlet on it's quite humid outside and could you just eat your bagel or it will be frozen stares all round.'

C.O.M.E.D.Y. Fun Facts

Henri Bergson wrote his seminal essays on laughter in 1900, and he remains one of the few philosophers to have addressed the topic of laughter with the comic as its source.

The three people who have come on the C.O.M.E.D.Y. Tour coo in consternation and proffer their tickets. Lucy, is wearing a fabulous red retro dress, wants to give comedy a go but isn't sure where and how to start. Ruth, known for quoting old Jewish jokes at family gatherings was gifted this tour for her seventieth birthday. And Andrew, thinning hair, dressed in black, wearing thick-rimmed spectacles is researching stand-up comedy for his next novel.

'C.O.M.E.D.Y. merchandise will be on sale throughout the tour but is not included in the price. There will be toilet breaks and food stops along the way. I hope that you enjoy the tour and ask that you take the time to rate it on Trip Advisor. And please follow the HA! HA! Flags, so that you don't get lost in the quagmire of invective that has been directed at funny women for a millennium.'

We begin the tour in a department store which is in keeping with the incongruity theory of laughter. You know, the idea that laughter is created because there is a difference between what we expect and what we get.[2]

As we enter the plush mirrored emporium, I grin at

C.O.M.E.D.Y. Fun Facts

Mikhail Bakhtin, the Russian linguist and literary critic writing in the first half of the twentieth century, used the term *carnivalesque* ***to distinguish writing that depicts the destabilisation or reversal of power structures in traditional forms of carnival, and by doing so subverts and liberates the assumptions of the dominant style or atmosphere through humour and chaos, particularly through bodily functions.***

The Group and say: 'No joking, I've read loads of Freud, Bergson and Bakhtin, three thinkers who have thought a lot about laughter. And I totally got the dissonance between humour and women, what with joke making being a power construct. A joke-teller must be assertive, self-assured and at times aggressive, and, really,' I say with my tongue firmly in my cheek, 'women should remain at the kitchen sink doing the dishes, dealing with the tidal wave of domestic detritus, and not get giddy about intruding on what has traditionally been men's business of generating the giggles, because, as Freud says: "There's a joke envelope, and the joke teller who undermines a person, idea or construct, thus elevating themselves as someone who is superior."[3] Similarly, Bergson, in his seminal essay on laughter (which surprisingly doesn't include the word *guffaw* in it, not even once) says that laughter is always at the expense of something. And joke-making, as ye olde town crier has decreed since time immemorial, is a man's dominion.

The purpose of laughter, as Bergson sees it, "is to humiliate, and consequently to correct our neighbour, if not in his will, at least in his deed."[4] So when a woman is funny, she must re-create the joke envelope, exert herself as someone who is powerful and, in turn, break the unspoken rules that associate her with silence and passivity.[5] Humour is, essentially, a network of inclusion and exclusion at the expense of the less powerful, and historically, women weren't meant to wield the power of humour because that would violate social conventions that champion a male point of view.'[6] Andrew makes notes in a small soft leather-bound notebook.

'So, let's for one crazy minute put a woman—you know the locus of all of that oozing and spurting, what with her ovaries and contemptible lactating ways—let's put her on stage. Her presence, of course, will cause the man in the audience to spray his pint of ale across the room, which he was quietly enjoying before he was faced with the spectre of a woman on stage, trying to make people laugh. As Mary Russo quite rightly says, a woman who is trying to make people laugh is just: "making a spectacle of herself" and showing off, and the danger with that, of course, is exposure. Men, as Russo asserts, expose themselves but that was something deliberate.[7] And we will look at a classic the exposure by Louis C.K., the darling of US comedy, who exposed himself without permission to women in his hotel room. When the women exposed Louis C.K. as part of the #metoo movement, Louis didn't take too kindly to it—but more on that later.'

As we enter the store, I guide The Group through the make-up department to a new stand that caters for the proliferation of hipsters who sport carnivalesque-style Ned Kelly beards.[8]

'Look at this,' I say, holding up a round silver tin with a 1950s-style cartoon of a man with a well-trimmed beard on the lid. 'This is The Bakhtin Beard wax. *"For the man who likes to wax lyrical".'* I give The Group a wry smile. 'Bakhtin observed that the upper part of the body is associated with cerebral functions and the lower part with life of the belly and reproductive organs, which are associated with filth and shame.[9]

The female body, as Mizejewski confirms, is seen as grotesque and this is at odds with the masculinised understanding of comedy.[10]And here,' I say widening my arms, to encompass all that is before us, the make-up, creams and potions, all offering the alluring promise of beautification, 'is a great place to talk about the female body being seen in a comedic context as grotesque. A woman is seen before she is heard and her primary functions of pregnancy, birth, lactation and menstruation are associated with shame and are therefore hidden. The function of comedy is to take charge, to be seen, and this is in part what has led to comedy being masculinised. Because women have traditionally been positioned into a place of passivity and therefore powerlessness, so, when a woman does perform comedy, she violates the patriarchal hegemony.

'There! I've used the word *hegemony*, so we can all relax now and know that we are in the hands of a skilled scholar. Where were we? Ah yes, women being seen before they are heard and the masculinisation of comedy not just as a performance, but also the descriptors of comedy: died, killed, bombed, has become the combative language of comedy, stampeding across the pages of men's books about humour and extoled by comedians for an eternity.

'Freud tells us that women have long been the butt of jokes.[11] So, if women want a piece of the side-splitting action, then the joke envelope needs to be reconstructed. The glue needs to come unstuck and be reapplied to the self-addressed envelope that a woman ought to send herself, to remind her that being a woman on stage, in front of a live audience is actually a magnificent act and something that a woman needs to give herself permission to do. Because, let's face it, humour has been held onto tightly for so long by men and, as Eliza Skinner in an article for the online platform *Refinery* quite rightly said, "Famous Dick Jokes are Just the Tip of the Problem".[12]

'But you know what women are like,' I nod to The Group. 'Women are sly, underhand witches who will wheedle their way into anything: board rooms, Australian Football League, and chat show panels. Next thing you know, they'll get some trumped-up idea and want to be Prime Minister! Sneaky, that's what women are. They'll stand up there on the stage, making it easy on the eye—but not too easy: we don't want that beer-spraying man to let an erection get in the way of a good joke.'

Andrew peers at me sceptically, rubs his unshaven face and quickly scans the ingredients on the back of the tin of Bakhtin Beard wax.

'Great gift for the Mandrew in your life.' I add.

'So you know how Phyllis Diller famously disguised her femininity by wearing shapeless garments, well that was to keep the attention on the comedy and off her body in order to make her presence on stage less offensive. [13] Historically, funny women have self-deprecated in order to signal to the men in the audience, to the man who introduced her, to the man who booked her, and to all of the men who perform before and after her, indicating that she knows she really shouldn't be there at all.' I say with a smirk.

'Any questions?' The Group shake their heads. 'Let's continue then,' I say. 'Let's go further into the department store and enter the "temporal modality of comedy which is a paradoxical continuity that builds and constructs (almost exclusively) with discontinuity, starting on one track and continuing on another as if it were completely natural".'[14]

Loop

'Oh look!' Cries Ruth pointing at a matt black display area adorned with an array of chunky jewellery. 'A Loop Stand. My daughter loves this jewellery. Have we got time for me to have a quick look?'

'Indeed we do.' I reply, 'And funnily enough I did a show at Melbourne International Comedy Festival one year and Loop was my muse, along with competitive home baking delivered in playgroups. The show was described as *'Radio National based comedy, dry yet engaging.'*

The *Loop* story based on the show is printed on tissue paper that is wrapped around Ruth's purchase. It is an indicator of how perishable and ephemeral joke telling is. It is there just for a shimmering moment.

Loop

'It happened about three months after the store opened.

We get together every week to have an array of interrupted conversations and chronicle the growth and development of our infants and toddlers. While some of us have pressed pause on high-flying careers to pop out a child or two, Ella and I are dreading going back to our jobs. Pre-kids, I'd worked in a low-paying job in the disability sector, and Ella sold handcrafted tie-dye cushions at markets, often waiting hours for a sale.

We're around the kitchen table, babies swaddled in their bassinet style car seats and toddlers playing outside. There is a fabulous assortment of home-baked items spread across the table. A fruit and chocolate loaf, a casual-but-stylishly-put-together platter of cheese, grilled bread and quince paste, and an assortment of semi-healthy muffins.

I learned to bake soon after the playgroup formed. When I first hosted playgroup, I swept the front of the massive porch on our double-fronted California bungalow, embarrassed that we didn't have a deck built out the back, a pronouncement that we weren't actually living the Australian Dream, we were just aspiring. In those early days of hosting, I presented VoVos, Mint Slices and Tim Tams unsheathed in their packets and arranged at diagonal angles on the dining table. But as the parade of home-baked items were whipped out one-by-one from underneath jogger strollers and prams, I hastily pushed the shop-bought biscuits to the back of the table. The icing on the cake, so to speak, was when Lizzy arrived with her three children, all under five years old, and presented an organic brown-flour banana bread, still warm from the oven, made with a recipe from Stephanie Alexander's The Cook's Companion.

Sanctimonious bitch, I thought as I fixed a smile of welcome, vowing then to learn how to make a slice at least, to present with aplomb when the need arose.

In the beginning, we'd share stories about everything; cracked nipples and embarrassing let-downs. When some of the kids started kinder, we progressed to eye-rolling, about why some of us get lumped with the fundraising activities: the mango drive, the ubiquitous chocolate drive, to help tackle childhood obesity and the begging of everyone you knew to come to the fundraising fete so that no child is without a laptop. Over numerous cups of tea, we'd lament our loss of self, the hazy memory of our work lives, and what we're planning to cook for dinner that night.

* * *

'So, when Drake latches on, it doesn't feel right,' declares Amanda, who had one of those nightmare births, an emergency C-section at the end of a forty-hour labour.

'Give us a look, maybe we can help,' Lottie suggests. She's a nurse, always offering up a diagnosis. She'd diagnose a dying plant.

'I'll get the puppies out then, shall I?' Amanda's red hair teems over the front of her engorged breasts. She releases a breast from her hammock-like bra trying to attach the squawking Drake. Her exposed alabaster flesh makes her look like a Botticelli painting.

We're all jostling for a spot to offer up advice. Our self-righteousness about lactation is as nauseating as morning sickness.

'Cup his head,' Lottie says.

'I'd just push his mouth on there,' advises Tessa, whose breasts are so little she repeatedly tells us, 'It's a wonder there's even one drop of milk in them.'

'Let him starve. If he's not going to latch on, then let him

starve till his mouth is so wide screaming that he can't do anything but latch on.' Alison has a string of no-nonsense pieces of instruction like this: from exactly how piles of washing should be transferred from surface to surface until they eventually make their way to the right drawer, to how many meals can be made in one week from minced meat. Alison is a schoolteacher and this approach is meted out to everyone equally, including her children. Truth be known, we're all a bit afraid of her.

Drake's squawk reaches a pitch that brings in all the children from outside. They're a raggedy bunch of toddlers, dressed in an assortment of brightly coloured clothes, fairy wings and gumboots. They charge through the door, bringing with them a trail of leaves, tiny pebbles and sticks collected from the pathway.

Ella pales visibly and yells at them: 'Drop everything and get out!'

Drake is now emitting a piercing sound, his face red. Amanda is weeping quietly.

'It's not worth it,' I say to her. 'It's just not worth it. Give him a bottle. You'll end up with mastitis, then be no good for anything.'

Amanda sniffs and tries once more to push Drake onto her swollen breast.

'We hungry,' says Zac, Lottie's youngest.

Ella gathers up sticks of celery and crackers, and an assortment of muffins. 'Sit here,' she says pointing to the back step. The toddlers sit together obediently and eat, like docile animals in a petting farm.

'Perhaps we should call it a day,' Lizzie says as she begins to gather up plates, cups and toys.

'Oh no, not this early!' Amanda cries. 'It'll be hours before Robbie comes home. I just can't stand the thought of an afternoon with this one and the toddler.' She caresses Drake's head. He's sucking noisily at her breast, making her wince.

Sometimes playgroup goes on for hours. Two is more than enough for me. The incessant drone about our respective partners, how little they help at home to how much sleep we crave but never get.

One time, after four hours at my place, I stiffly asked everyone to leave, using the 'I have things to do' line.'Oh yes of course we're going,' they all chorused at once. 'We totally forgot the time.'

How they can forget the time is beyond me. Our whole lives are dictated by our children's demands on our time: feeding, sleeping, washing, cooking for them. Standing in parks for an eternity, pushing swings and uttering onomatopoeic words when a child goes down a slide or jiggles on a seesaw. 'Whoosh, wee eeh aw, ee aw.'

It's all so boring that never once have I managed to forget the time. I'm always glancing at my phone, contemplating how long it will be before I can get away from the park, estimating how long it will take to get to the supermarket, how long it will take my son Jacob to eat his lunch. How long everything seems to take, and yet how little time I have to do anything of any merit beyond washing a load of laundry or a pile of dishes.

'Why don't we go out?' Lottie said once. 'You know, just around the block. It will be fun!' No one ever wants to, though. No one wants to meet at a park, where you could leave when you want and wouldn't have to worry about the dishes. It's always at each other's houses, where some appear not to mind the mess of toddlers and appear genuinely interested in absolutely everything we mothers have to say.

So it's a complete surprise when Ella says, 'Let's go to Loop.'

'Loop?' asks Lizzy, 'That new jewellery store on the corner? What on earth for, and with this lot?' She gestures to the toddlers.

'Come on,' says Ella, 'It'll be a fun outing, and it's only around the corner. Come on.'

The children are gathered, and prams are packed. It's all slightly shambolic. Amanda rubs her breasts as she packs up nappies, wipes milk from the infant's face and puts her toddler into the pram. I nudge her.

'Bottle feed him, please. Stop trying to be a hero about this.'

Amanda looks at me sharply. 'Leave it, Julia. Just leave it.'

Embarrassed by Amanda's terse response, I quickly pick up my now-grubby toddler. I wipe down his hands and face, then cajole him into the pram by bribing him with another muffin.

We look like a flotilla for the Moomba parade as we head along Plenty Road towards Loop. Lizzy and Lottie are chattering about a trip to Noosa that they have planned for the end of the year. Ella and Amanda are laughing at their toddlers trying to push sultanas up their noses. Alison is droning on about her lack of energy and how she hates the way her hair turned fuzzy after the birth of her third child.

The tagline emblazoned on Loop's window is: Designed right here, handmade globally. We all know it's baloney, but people flock anyway.

The shop bell rings repeatedly as we hold the doors open and pull and push our prams into the slick store. I'm already wondering what possessed us all to come here with this ragtag bunch of toddlers and infants.

The store is filled with moulded jewellery in muted reds, greys and greens. Within weeks of the store opening, chunky-shaped birds, beads, frosted glass pendants and bracelets were seen dangling on the arms, necks and ears of women throughout the northern suburbs who worked with 'the community,' in the not-for-profit sector or local government.

Earrings are held up and compliments uttered is a world away from the mayhem of playgroup. The shh, shh of the smoothly-opening drawers that store the treasured items is like a calming soundtrack.

Periodically, some of us go over to jostle the prams in an effort to placate irritable infants.

Some of us try on overpriced baggy jumpers and floaty-sleeved garments, others purchase discounted bracelets and remark about the shoes and bags that they love but won't buy.

The shop assistant is watchful as some of the toddlers try to wrestle free of their restraints. Drake begins to do his cough-cough sound working up to a cry.

Amanda sighs and says, 'Oh well, it was nice, but I suppose

I should go.'

A damp patch is forming on her blouse front. 'Time to get a compress on this.' She lugs her limousine-style pram out the door, smiles thinly and mutters 'It's my turn to host next week. See you all then.'

She clicks the door shut, and we hear Drake's squawk rising above the rattle of a passing tram.

We all begin to leave reluctantly, knowing that waiting for us back home is another pile of washing, another cup of tea that will go cold before it's drunk and the vague idea of 'something nice' for dinner.

Lizzy, Alison and Lottie head off together. They live within minutes of each other and often go to each other's homes outside of the playgroup meetings.

Ella and I are the last to leave the shop. On the footpath, I smile at Ella and say, 'This Loop jewellery is spreading like a rash through the northern suburbs. I reckon it'll be the new Tupperware party for desperate mums wanting to make a buck.'

I get out the earrings I've bought, confessing that I'll probably never wear them, 'because everyone is', gesturing a faux yawn of contempt.

I put the felt bag holding the jewellery into my bag and am about to make another quip about felt being the new macramé when Ella, her face blushing, says: 'I'm starting work there next week. I love that store and it's a proper job, my first bloody proper job since dropping out of uni'.

I begin backpedalling. 'Oh Ella, it's lovely jewellery. It's just not for me. It's just not my style'

I see Ella's hands clench on the pram handle, her son Clyde squirming to get out.

'I thought you, out of everyone, wouldn't judge me for working there. For working in a shop, instead of being an academic, or having a well-paid job in local government. I thought you would understand.'

She wheels the pram around and leaves. My cheeks are burning, no doubt as red as the earrings rammed into the basket under the stroller. Another tram rattles by.

'Go home! Go home! Go home!' Jacob shouts at me, his face smeared in food and his legs kicking against the footrest of the stroller.

* * *

A week later, we gather at Amanda's. I try to catch Ella's eye, but she fusses over her home-made zucchini slice and begins an intense conversation with Lizzie and Lottie about a children's play event they took their kids to at Art Play.

Suddenly there is a thud from one of the rooms off the hallway, then a cry. The pitch of the cry is such that we all instinctively move towards the bedroom. As if lined up for an inspection, the rag tag group of toddlers, eyes downcast stare at a pool of liquid leaching from a damaged pink ukulele on the edge of a red Persian rug.

The toddlers begin to chatter at once, some pointing, some crying. Jacob is pointing to Clyde, who is red-faced, crying and shouting, 'Not, not, not me.'

'Clyde did wee wee mummy, in the ukulele.' Jacob's voice is a whisper, one hand close to his mouth ready to suck his thumb, the other pointing to the impossibly large puddle next to the offending ukulele.

'That's it!' screamed Amanda, her voice matching Drake's earlier squawks. 'That's it—playgroup is over. Everyone get out!'

Gender Trouble

I guide The Group from the Loop stand to the elevator and tell them, 'We're going to the basement now. You know, that badass place where women-be-damned for having the impudence to rip off their aprons and for wanting to be *seen* outside of the province of domesticity. Judith Butler's in charge of this floor because, as suggested by the title of one of her books, *Gender Trouble,* gender is a matter of interpellation, a process of encountering cultural values and internalising them as something we must accept and reiterate in daily performance; something we say 'yes' to.'

Muzak plays as we enter the bedding and homewares department. Judith Butler beckons us over to where she is leaning next to a bed made up with Egyptian cotton sheets that are on sale, have a 1000 thread count and create a luxury, plush sleeping experience every night. Judith's hand ruffles through her salt-and-pepper hair as she intones, 'All gender is performed. Gender itself is a constructed identity'.[15]

Everyone in The Group places their chins on their hands and frowns a little, each wanting to look learned to truly understand what Judith means.

Judith continues: 'Feminist theory has often been critical of the naturalistic explanations of sex and sexuality that assume the meaning of women's social existence can be derived from some fact of their physiology.'[16]

She pauses, her hand skimming over a plumped-up pillow covered in the aforementioned Egyptian cotton with the impossibly high thread count. 'Gender then, can be neither true nor false, neither real nor apparent. And yet, one is compelled to live in a world in which genders constitute univocal signifiers, in which gender is stabilized, polarized, rendered discrete and intractable. In effect, gender is made to comply with a model of truth and falsity which not only contradicts its own performative fluidity but serves a social policy of gender regulation and control. Performing one's gender wrong initiates a set of punishments both obvious and indirect, and performing it well provides the reassurance that there is an essentialism of gender identity after all.'[17]

Judith nods to Ruth who has put her hand up. 'So when a woman does stand-up comedy, it's not just a question of whether she's funny or not, but more that she has not complied with what is expected of her.'

Judith smiles her wry smile. 'The thing is, gender is not passively scripted on the body, and neither is it determined by nature, language, the symbolic, or overwhelming history of patriarchy. Gender is what is put on, invariably under constraint, daily and incessantly, with anxiety and pleasure.'[18]

Andrew scribbles more notes in his book.

'So, does that then mean when a woman gets up on stage, she is refusing to be complicit in what is expected of her as a woman?' Ruth asks, while paying for a set of the Egyptian cotton sheets. 'Such a good price, it seems a shame not too.'

Judith replies, signing her autograph on Ruth's receipt: 'The fallacy of the notion of gender is that it is learned, imposed upon us.'[19] Think of it like a gender reveal party hosted by woke folk, who decorate their house with streamers printed with the words *The Joke's on You. We don't go for pink or blue because gender is just a social construct.* The Group laughs. 'Thanks for dropping by, enjoy the rest of your C.O.M.E.D.Y. Tour,' Judith says as she waves goodbye.

'She's a lot taller than I thought she would be,' Lucy says to Ruth, who agrees. The Group enters the lift and we go up a level.

'Did you get that?', I ask The Group. 'What Judith was saying is that when a woman gets on stage, she is imperfectly repeating her gender within a binary framework, and comedy has long been seen in a binary framework. So, when the recipient of the joke is a man and the joke-teller is a woman, then the joke contract must be re-aligned, so, for that to work, women have employed a variety of methods to disguise not just their sexuality, but also their comedic material, in order to perform in a comedic framework, and each time women perform, they move away from the ideal of what is expected of her as woman. To fully understand that let's go to the haberdashery and homewares department.

'If you need a toilet break now is your chance. When

you're done we'll stop at the café for a single origin Madagascan drip filter coffee and listen to a reading of a short story based on my Melbourne International Comedy Festival show, called *Snore.*'

We stir our coffees and the story begins:

Doreen

'Brian.' Doreen moans, head tilted, legs flaying, back arched.

'Brian!' This time it sounds like the word 'Bran' but said loudly and angrily, in a tone not usually applied to breakfast cereal.

Doreen's fingernails clutch the sides of the bed. Her lament, her arched back, the yelling of the name of the man lying next to her are not, however, to be confused with that of a woman in the throes of passion.

'Brian!' Doreen's pitch rises now to meet her husband's increasingly thunderous nocturnal nasal noises. She makes contact with Brian's body, by way of a short sharp kick to the calf. This elicits a brief braying noise replaced by the rhythmic snore which habitually interrupts Doreen's sleep.

Her toes wriggle into maroon slippers at the side of the bed. She stands, then crashes back onto the bed vengefully, willing Brian's snoring to end and wishing she could go back to sleep. The futility of the wish leaves her fuming. She leaves the bedroom, harrumphing, slamming the door. The nocturnal nasal noises pause momentarily, then settle once more into their regular rumbling inhalation and lip flapping exhalation.

She edges along the dark passageway, her forget-me-not floral nightdress ballooning around her legs. She pulls out a pink and cream checked blanket from the linen closet, then makes her way to the living room.

The golden tassels of the lampshade ripple like a 1920's flapper dancer's dress. On top of the cabinet there are clusters of photographs; the cousins from County Cork, a brother now long dead, his wife and adult children, all sitting politely on chairs and staring unsmiling at the camera, and an array of family weddings, the dresses getting shorter through the 1960s and 70s then lengthening again in the 80s. Dozens of passport-sized images with bright blue backgrounds and gap-toothed grins of the countless nieces and nephews, sent every year inside a Christmas card with a perfunctory greeting.

When Doreen does the dusting on a Tuesday, her hands hover over a sepia image of a man in army fatigues, his eyes averted from the camera, a soft shadow of a smile playing on his lips.

Inside the cabinet is a collection of silver bells and commemorative plates from the Royal family's silver jubilees and weddings, china plates and teacups used only on special occasions and next to them a half-filled crystal decanter of Harvey's Bristol Cream Sherry.

Doreen is hunched by the weight of the pink and cream blanket draped around her shoulders. Her lips are pursed, her nightie rucked up around her knees. The blood is pooling in her veins around her ankles making her skin look like Stilton cheese.

A dog's distant bark and the hum of the fridge are the only sounds. Doreen leans on the pouchy armrests of the floral armchair, her back just touching the neatly arranged cushions. She stares fixedly in front of her, the skin on her neck tensing, then relaxing. She is silent for a very long time, then exhales loudly. 'Thirty,' she says. 'I've done thirty.' She looks down at her belly, as if to inspect her efforts, sighs and declares to the room, 'There, I've done me thirty pelvic floors.'

She is a short woman. Trim, she thinks, quite trim. Not like Brian, who has let himself go. The pints of ale, the sedentary bank job, the short walks to and from the bus stop every morning his only movement, and the result a protruding belly like a pregnancy in its final trimester.

Doreen takes her glasses from their case, grey and heavily rimmed, jam jar-bottomed in their density. She picks up a Woman's Weekly *from the magazine rack, flicks through it and stops to inspect a picture of a woman who admits she has had work done.*

Doreen looks down at herself, pushes her chin into her chest, then drags the flesh upwards to de-crepe her neck. She repeats the action several times. Not satisfied with that, she pulls the flesh from below her eyes and gathers it downwards to un-wrinkle her face. She stretches her jaw open and shut, then lets her shoulders sag as if resigned to the continual downward drift of everything.

She reaches into her knitting bag, embroidered with a cottage scene. From its depths, she pulls out a handful of toffees. Her jaws begin to work on the confectionery. She licks some drool from the bottom corner of her lip. The addition of a second toffee slows down the chewing motion. She pushes another one in, which makes her cheek bulge.

She takes the wrappers, flattens them on her knee, and holds one at arm's length as if inspecting a rare item like an assessor on Antiques Roadshow. She swallows, and reads, 'Who am I?'

Her jaw slackens and, as if unable to answer the question empty-mouthed, she stuffs in three more toffees. Her jaw stiffens with the effort. She slurps as a rogue bit of sugary saliva runs from the side of her mouth.

'Oungh,' she purrs, 'Oungh. Who am I?' Born in Melbourne in 1968, known for my television role, but more so for my singing. 'Oungh' she tuts quietly, 'I'm Kylie Minogue.'

Doreen holds out the wrapper which confirms her answer.

Who am I?

'Barry Humphries.'

'Sir Elton John.'

'Joan Collins.'

The answers are reeled off as the toffees are chewed and teeth picked clean of confection.

She counts fourteen wrappers and considers that it's not as many as Tuesday, but more than Thursday. Then she pushes them under the rose-patterned cushion. Brian wouldn't venture beneath the cushions, his domain is the lawn, but the pat is reassuring, nevertheless.

Doreen remembers the day she stood out there on Brian's lawn one Sunday, looking at the patterns that the mower had made, just waiting there alongside the garden gnome. She was there because Brian had taken it upon himself to make the gravy, out of the blue, not so much as a 'by your leave'. He'd just got up off the chair from reading the Sunday paper, calm as you like and said, 'I'll make the gravy today.'

Just stood up, strode across the kitchen linoleum, all how's your father?

'I'll make the gravy,' he'd said. Like that's what he did every week.

What possessed him, she'll never know. He'd got the box of Gravox down from the cupboard, scraped the meat juice from the bottom of the pan and stirred it and stirred it. She wouldn't have minded if this is what he normally did, but it wasn't. She had looked pointedly at him while he'd stirred, wearing the expression she'd normally use for having too much loose change in her purse. But it didn't work. So, she'd tried the expression she'd used that time after Aunt Peggy's funeral.

After the funeral, in the church hall, Joan Hampshire, the woman from O'Keefe Street, had come in all organised, with a pavlova base, cream already whipped in a bowl and holding what everyone had assumed to be a tin of passionfruit for the top.

But out of nowhere, Joan had pulled three peppermint crisp bars from her bag and smashed them with a rolling pin. Lord only knows where that had come from. Who brings a rolling pin to a funeral? There she was though, bold as brass, with her three peppermint crisp bars, a rolling pin, a shop-bought pavlova base and some whipped cream. At a wake.

Doreen had pulled her lips tight, flared her nostrils, jutted her chin out. Then she'd made a braying noise, pushing the air out of her nose, quickly. She assumed that this would have had an effect on Joan. But Joan had acted like it was the most natural thing in the world, standing there making a peppermint crisp pavlova at a wake. Never mind that there were forty-five of Louise Dalgetty's scones already waiting to be eaten.

Though the expression hadn't worked that day on Joan, Doreen's neighbour—Stella—with her arms folded, lips pressed, eyebrows raised, had given her a quick nod of approval.

Doreen had pulled out that expression the day that Brian had made the gravy. But it had made no difference. Brian had even whistled while he stirred. Doreen had stood out there in the garden. She'd had to leave the kitchen there and then, just to get a breath of fresh air, she'd even left her pinny on, gone outside and stood next to the garden gnome, its nose bulbous, its gut protruding, not unlike Brian, she'd thought at the time.

They didn't speak about it over the roast dinner, which, truth-be-known, was a bit stringy that day.

The golden carriage clock ticks 4.05 am. Doreen divests herself from the pink chequered blanket and walks towards the peachy velvet drapes, deckled by a pleated pelmet. Her hand touches a fold in the curtain and flinches as if it might be hot. She waits, parts it a fraction, and peers out. The lawn looks black and the privet hedge, cut low, like a solid brick wall in the dim light. Doreen notes that the rubbish bin is still out at number 51. She shakes her head in contempt. A rubbish bin left out all night after bin collection. The gall of it, she thinks, the absolute gall of it.

The dawn is just about to break through on Grand Final Day and Doreen wonders, as she peers through the crack of the curtain, if there will be a repeat of last year's events.

At 4.35 am, the light in the kitchen of number 45 goes on. Doreen shrinks back for fear of being seen, a sickly feeling rising in her, unrelated to her recent toffee consumption.

Her neighbours, Stella and Frank, had come over last year on Grand Final Day, like they always did. Coleslaw with low-fat dressing was in the faux crystal bowl that she and Brian had got for their wedding. Buttered rolls were piled high, ready for Doreen's rissoles. Brian and Frank had stood around drinking beers out of tins. Grand Final made people do things like that, act all relaxed and do away with niceties. Brian had a flush on him from the beer, she could see it spreading up his neck. He'd done away with his tie at the last minute, too. Not like him, but he had. He was telling Frank about the goldfish, his head going round and round as if he could see it still in its bowl, his hand imitating the sprinkling motion of feeding it. Frank had laughed—unkindly, thought Doreen—when Brian moved on to the bit where the fish had died.

Doreen could still see Brian now, stooped down over the azaleas, head bowed, trowel in hand, lips moving as he scattered the earth over the dead fish.

After Brian had told Frank the story, Stella and Doreen had gone inside to prepare lunch. The rissoles were made the night before and Stella had put her crouton and bacon salad on the table, waiting until just before they ate to add the dressing.

Dessert was always made on the day. Grand Final Day dessert was Doreen's specialty.

'He never did recover from the fish,' Doreen had told Stella, as she began getting ingredients from the pantry: coconut, Marie biscuits, sweetened condensed milk, butter, a lemon, and the grater from the stove top. Though she hardly needed the recipe, she had pulled down the worn and battered copy of her Woman's Weekly cookbook anyway.

As Doreen leaned against the bench and began crushing the biscuits, Stella came up right behind her. Doreen could feel her breath on her neck and smell her Avon moisturizer. It had made her feel quite disorientated, having Stella stand so close to her.

Then, Stella had put her hand quickly around the side of Doreen's face, and quite suddenly, Doreen could not see a thing.

She realised she was blindfolded with Brian's blue tie, the one with the white diagonal stripe, the one he'd left on the back of the kitchen door.

'Make it now,' Stella said, right in Doreen's ear.

'You're always saying you can "mek it with your eyes closed".' Stella said.

Doreen's hands began to ache from crushing the biscuits under circumstances she had never imagined, when suddenly the bowl was pushed just beyond her reach. Her hands searched frantically across the kitchen bench for the bowl of half-crushed Marie biscuits, but to no avail.

No expression in her arsenal seemed the right one to use

this time. Her mouth was rippling trying to find one. She couldn't use the one for when she was waiting at the butcher's in a long line and certainly not the expression she used when she was at the bus stop in the rain. So, she began to protest, her mouth wide, not unlike Frank's dying fish, she thought fleetingly.

As she inhaled, ready to shout, she felt the tips of Stella's fingers, probing at first, then plunging inwards. And not just one finger either, but four of them, filling her mouth. Her tongue softened and her jaw went slack as Stella's four fingers, sopped in sweetened condescend milk, filled her mouth with loveliness.

Now, Doreen had pleasured Brian hundreds of times over the years, but nothing could have prepared her for Stella's four fingers covered in sweetened condensed milk, plunged into the depths of her mouth.

They stayed like that for a while, Stella's breath warm on her face, Doreen's tongue suckling Stella's four fingers, saliva spilling from the sides of her mouth. It had made Doreen think of things that she'd never thought about before, like what Stella's hair would feel like. It looked stiff because she used a lot of hairspray, but maybe it wasn't.

Doreen's mind was just drifting to the idea of what Stella's hair stiff with spray would feel like when Stella chuckled removed the blindfold, her fingers dabbing away a stream saliva from of Doreen's chin.

Doreen had not been able to look Stella in the eye after the blindfold was removed and she'd busied herself, finishing off the lemon slice, pressing it into the tray, noting that the level was lower than usual. Stella went out to where Brian and Frank were sitting and gathered up dishes, brought them back in like it was just another Saturday.

That Grand Final Day, the rissoles were a little burnt, Brian's blue tie had to be washed and Stella, Frank, and of course Brian had complimented Doreen on the deliciousness of her lemon slice. And Doreen had drunk more than one glass of the Harvey's Bristol cream sherry from the china cabinet.

The shock of what happened that day had never left Doreen. She had re-enacted it at times, wrapping the tie around her head and peeking through the underside, noticing that her jaw dropped, her eyes softened and her lips moistened from the constant licking.

Doreen shakes herself from her reverie and goes towards the window to pull back the curtain. In the yellow pool of light at the kitchen table of number 47, Doreen sees Stella seated at her kitchen table, her eyes cast downwards, the fingers on her right hand slowly running up and down the length of an unopened packet of Marie biscuits.

The Group chuckle and we move on.

Droll Dolls

The lift doors open onto a vast array of homewares, tchotchkes and Hallmark cards—you know the kind of thing: *'The joke represents a rebellion against authority.'*[20] *so make people laugh and have a great birthday already*. Next to the cards is an assortment of joke envelopes in a startling array of colours, signifying the vast array of joke-telling techniques. The words *Mixed Bill* flash in crimson neon lights over a set of Gorman patterned tea-towels. The scent of bergamot, geranium and peppercorn wafts up from vats of propitiating salve. Printed on the label are the words: *The Propitiating Salve has been made specially for the C.O.M.E.D.Y. Tour and offers skin toughening qualities—a must for all aspiring comics, especially women.*

'Oh, this smells lovely,' Lucy declares, rubbing the salve into her hands and up the length of her exposed arms. She takes the 500 ml pump pack to the purchase desk and Ruth compliments her on her choice, saying it is the equivalent of buying garlic to ward off vampires.

I lead The Group over to a newly arrived shipment of C.O.M.E.D.Y Tour merchandise. A ripple of amusement goes through them, and shouts of 'Look at this one', and 'This one's my favourite' resound.

The display area is filled with Droll Dolls, a collection of miniature replicas of female comedians who have used self-deprecation because this was their only means of defence, given sociocultural parameters.[21]

'The Droll Dolls,' I tell The Group, 'are manufactured by a social enterprise collective, run by a group of highly skilled migrant women who were taking part in a compulsory settlement program. The women shunned the idea of training to become childcare and aged care workers because they were empowered by a 'speak out' component of the program which taught the basics of stand-up comedy. From there, they researched representation of women in the stand-up comedy industry and created the Droll Dolls. Initially the dolls were hand-crafted and sold at markets, then they upscaled to manufactured figurines made from discarded Barbie Dolls. The Droll Doll enterprise has been hugely successful, with orders coming in from all parts of the globe.'

Lucy holds up a Phyllis Diller Droll Doll, which is sporting a flouncy oversized dress and a whacky hairdo. I tell The Group: 'The Droll Doll collective has painstakingly researched the history of gender and humour, and the Droll Dolls represent the changing nature of self-deprecation. Self-deprecation has been used as a comedic device, challenging the status quo but also affirming it depending on how it is used and received by the audience. The Droll Doll Collective employs only women and pays above-award wages. It's very difficult to get large department stores to stock their goods, so, really, it's an incredible outcome that The Department Store is stocking them. And the Droll Dolls themselves, well, as you can see, they are stunning.'

I gesture grandly at the array of Droll Dolls and say: 'Let's look at the Phyllis Diller Doll, so that we can understand why female comedians historically used self-deprecation. And of course marvel at the loveliness of the Droll Dolls themselves. Diller's self-deprecatory material may appear demeaning (towards herself and/or women in general), but closer scrutiny reveals that Diller's jokes accomplished what all marginal humour accomplishes—they call cultural values into question by lampooning them.'[22] The power of comedy is that it can question values and assumptions, and that by laughing, we acknowledge the absurdity of them.

'And,' I say, 'each Doll talks—they have been given a voice!' At the press of a button, Diller's voice pipes out: 'I was the world's ugliest baby. When I was born, the doctor slapped everybody.'[23]

'And, whilst this is a classic line, it is also an example of the instability of self-deprecation. One person might read this is a demeaning joke. Another might read it as

C.O.M.E.D.Y. Fun Facts

Bridgette Christie dressed as an ant to show the absurdity of discriminating against women in comedy.[30]

subverting the expectations that all babies are praised as beautiful (even when they're not).'

The Group clamour over the Droll Dolls. 'Such great gift ideas, I'm going to get this one for my granddaughter's Bat Mitzvah,' Ruth says as she picks up the Joan Rivers Droll Doll. It has a moulded nose, a shock of blonde hair and a range of accessories sold separately. Ruth laughs as Joan's twangy voice declares: 'My breasts are so low, now I can have a mammogram and a pedicure at the same time.'[24]

'The information on the back of the packaging, along with providing the age-appropriateness of the Doll (from birth upwards), advises that: 'Joan Rivers had a comedy career spanning more than five decades. Her humour was aggressive in tone and content. This aggression was directed towards either herself or the audience through the use of self-deprecating comedy. The comedy lies in River's actual appearance and her self-perception, making the woman on stage more palatable for those audience members who may feel threatened by seeing a woman on stage.'[25] This also leaves the audience questioning what Rivers thinks of herself—does she see herself as being more, or less, beautiful than she is?'

I tell The Group: 'In order to be able to perform, women initially employed self-deprecation, as a way of acknowledging they were somewhere that was not considered their domain. Women used self-deprecation to undermine themselves as the joke-teller, in order to achieve a level of acceptance and to put the audience at ease. "Self-deprecation eases the resistance to the idea of a female comic. The logic being that if a woman is doing something that they aren't supposed to do then they might be more acceptable if they show that they don't think much of them self in the first place."[26]'

'Look,' I say to The Group, 'The Droll Dolls are arranged in chronological order, highlighting the changing nature of self-deprecation and how women initially adapted their comedic voices to align with traditional masculine comedic traits as well as creating comedy on their own terms. Self-deprecation is a way of not just reinforcing gender types or playing out what is expected of a comic but is also a tool of reassurance—and the reassurance that self-deprecatory jokes can provide is significant. Comedy can express failure to conform to body norms or gender stereotypes, providing acknowledgement and validation that these issues and feelings of inadequacy exist. Any self-deprecatory utterance in live comedy performance will always simultaneously both reinforce and challenge hegemonic views of women and their bodies.[27] And comedy is an excellent way in which a woman can reflect the absurdity of the dominant ideology while undermining the very basis for its discourse.[28]

'So, if you look along the line of Droll Dolls starting in the 1950s with Diller and Rivers, then move on to the last decade, you can see a huge shift not just in the number of female comedians, but also in the changing nature of self-deprecation and how women now do comedy differently to their predecessors. You can also see the way that women have used their bodies and sexuality as an integral part of their comedy. As Russo notes, "the reintroduction of the body and categories of the body into the realm of the political has been a central concern of feminism".[29] And comedy has grown up alongside each successive wave of feminism, so can be linked with emancipation and women being seen and heard in the public domain.'

I hold up the Bridget Christie Droll Doll. 'Here you can see Christie, a UK feminist comedian, dressed as an ant, complete with swimming goggles, pipe cleaner antennae and a striped tie to indicate that she was a *professional comedian*. The costume is a replica of the one she wore in her show *Ant* at the 2010 Edinburgh Fringe Festival.[30] Christie dressed as an ant because, as she said: "When I started doing comedy, in 2006, attitudes towards female comics were much worse than they are now. It's much better now there are more of us, but sometimes back then, the disappointment caused by the arrival of my point of view and X chromosomes on stage, was palpable. How I got round it was by dressing as an ant and addressing how absurd it was to be singled out because of one's sex."[31]'

I press the Christie Droll Doll and she quips: 'It's different now, in the '80s, you'd be lucky to see one ant on the bill, let alone three or four.'[32]

'The Christie Doll,' I tell The Group, 'is doing something different to Diller and Rivers. Christie self-deprecates by disguising her body in order to highlight the absurdity of thinking about sexuality and bodies in the first place, when defining who can and can't be funny. This shows that when self-deprecation is strategic, its subversive effect may be to send a subtle double message, at times becoming a type of embodiment of the power of the powerless.[33]

'Earlier on the C.O.M.E.D.Y. Tour, I mentioned Bakhtin in reference to the abhorrence of seeing a woman on stage and the connection to bodily fluids, thus making a woman less appealing than a man doing comedy. This is because a man's presence is associated with cerebral function and not bodily fluids that are perceived as grotesque, which is a great segue into two comedians who, playing on their femininity rather than denying or undermining it, talk about their bodily functions, their unapologetic desire for sex, and their bodies as objects of desire.'

I hold up the Amy Schumer and Sarah Silverman Droll Dolls. Sarah is casually dressed in cut-off denim shorts and a hoody, and Amy's long blonde hair cascades over a slinky red dress worn with strappy heels.

'What Silverman and Schumer's comedy represents is a progression of what has come before them. Silverman echoes Lenny Bruce's propensity to shock audiences for the purposes of making a serious moral point using her gender and ethnicity as a way to articulate her humour.[34] What Schumer and Silverman both do—unlike their male Jewish comedy counterparts whose comedy focuses on anxiety and their Jewishness—is keep their Jewishness strategically within parentheses, neither denying it nor completely ignoring it. Instead, they engage with it purposefully without ever allowing it to eclipse the other components of their humour or personae.[35] Schumer and Silverman enact their Jewishness by acting like 'men'. They joke openly and in great detail about sex, their enjoyment of sex, and their bodies, and they make extensive use of profanity. I call this 'The Esther Effect', from the biblical story of Esther who had to hide her Judaism until she revealed it as an act of bravery. Esther is celebrated in the festival of Purim which is a raucous celebration of drinking and dressing up. Silverman's and Schumer's Jewishness—and I would also say femininity—is used strategically, when it is called upon, and it brings with it a great lexicon of collective knowledge and prejudices about Jews.

'It is interesting to note how Silverman uses shock as a way of calling out moral issues and doesn't use self-deprecation in the way other comedians use: she is unapologetic about being on stage. Listen to what the Silverman Droll Doll says "I was raped by a doctor, which is a bittersweet experience for a Jewish girl."[36] It adds a dark twist to the stereotypical Jewish family expectations that a Jewish woman should either marry a doctor or become one.

'Silverman puts equal weighting across the material. This kind of joke-telling is a statement that is funny and thought-provoking all at once, playing on the idea of types that we know and are familiar with, that don't require laborious introductions or descriptions. This joke is made up of fifteen words and demonstrates the exquisite beauty of comedy: a brevity of language. Excellent joke-making is the ability to say so little and yet so much while making people laugh and think.

'It's so great to see comedians like Silverman and Schumer do comedy. Their style is just so unapologetic they lay claim to what I call a 'mirthful mutiny', whereby they take on male traits of comedy but also wholeheartedly talk about their bodies and sex in a raunchy and really clever way. "Schumer can be justifiably viewed as part of a revolution in feminist performance in their embracing of women's sexuality and pleasure without euphemism, in talking openly about how they feel about their bodies, and in calling out the misogyny that openly targets them directly."[37]'

'Let's listen to what Schumer has to say.' I press the Doll: "I get labelled a sex comic. But if a guy got up on stage and pulled his dick out, everybody would say: 'He's a thinker."[38]'

'A personal favourite of mine,' I tell The Group, 'is the *Marvellous Mrs Maisel* Droll Doll.'

'Oh, I loved that show!' Ruth exclaims. 'The make-up and the costumes alone were stunning. And the episodes set in the Catskills, oh my.

'Indeed!' I reply. 'The premise of the *Marvellous Mrs Maisel* show is fabulous. Mrs Maisel—Midge—is the female equivalent of the US comedian, Lenny Bruce. Mrs Maisel performs alongside Lenny, breaking as many rules as Lenny does. But, unlike Mrs Maisel's female comedic contemporaries of the 1950s, Mrs Maisel does not disguise her femininity—she celebrates it. Nor does she use self-deprecation as a technique to apologise or excuse her presence on stage. And look at the costume this Doll's wearing! It's magnificent. The hair, the lipstick stunning. And listen.' I press the button for The Group to hear: "Comedy is fuelled by oppression, by lack of power, by sadness and disappointment, by abandonment and humiliation. Now, who the hell does that describe more than women? Judging by those standards, only women should be funny."[39]

Oy to the Vey!

'Oooh look a bagel cart!' Ruth points to a mobile bagel cart being pushed through the store by a female Rabbi from the North.

'Ah ha!' I say. 'Fabulous right on time. This is our morning tea, provided by the Great Synagogue of the North, where a gender neutral shabbat is all the go. This is the perfect time to talk about Jewish humour. We can't talk about comedy and not talk about Jews.'

The Rabbi smiles and encourages The Group to choose from a tantalising array of freshly made bagels, filled with smoked salmon, cream cheese and dill.

'Ah Rabbi,' I say, 'At last a kosher bagel cart on the North Side.'

'Yes, the Bagel Belt has widened its girth. No longer can the Southside claim that they are the purveyors of the best bagels in Melbourne.'

'So, Jews and humour. Do you agree that it's in our DNA, with the unenviable the mix of pogroms, persecution which translates to punchlines right?'

'Indeed Jews and humour have long been synonymous and the advent of stand-up comedy as we know it today via the Catskills in New York.

Jews of New York vacationed in the Catskill Mountains for many years. Their influence in the region is so significant that the area became known as the Borscht Belt. There was a captive audience and with that the need to entertain people—and so it began—the birth of modern stand up as we know it—predominantly men—telling jokes.

Catskills comedians made jokes insulting their in-laws, their wives or members of the audience and it wasn't until the post war era with comedians like Lenny Bruce and Mort Sahl that comedy began to challenge the status quo questioning assumptions about race, gender, and communism.

Anthropologist Stephanie Koziski described the role of the post-war comedian, she wrote: 'Comedian's routines are like myths in primitive cultures helping to deliver explanations of good and evil in the human experience, offering a way to manage fear and anxiety by admonishing social chaos. Post-war comedians pushed comedic boundaries set by the Catskill circuit, and heightened America's awareness of their political and social surroundings. Comedy had become a tool for social protest.'

By the late 70's Jews and stand-up comedy became synonymous—because as *Time* magazine noted that although Jews constituted only 3% of the U.S. population, 80% of the nation's professional comedians were Jewish. This also coincided with the Yiddishization of American comedy Jewish comedic themes and strategies informed stand-up comedy, and the Jewish comedian's influence was so effective that the new brand of comedy that developed during the 1950s projected a Jewish identity upon the American public.

US psychologist Samuel Janus spent ten years researching Jews and comedy, interviewing 76 comics and said what makes Jewish comics funny 'is their pain'. He claimed Jews dominated the American comedic industry because of their outsider status in American culture, and they used comedy as a defence mechanism to ward off the aggression and hostility of others. Jews,' he said, 'have used humour as a weapon against oppression.'

In context to comedy being a survival mechanism —I don't know of any other religion or culture that has so many holidays, rituals and foods to remind us that someone tried to kill us, but despite the pogroms and persecution we survived.

In Australia unlike America, everyone is othered, besides the cis gendered white male, there is not a dominant ethnic voice here.

Comedy as a power construct can be traced back to philosophers Aristotle and Plato who saw comedy as a mechanism which creates a sense of superiority and has the ability to undermine social structures. Comedians have a licence to speak about matters that in many other contexts would not be permissible. In some instances, comedians say what we are all thinking but dare not say.

And comedy as satire is a parody of power. If there's just anger, it doesn't work. Anger and funny, that works. Comedy can do the heavy lifting. Comedy can tackle anything, even teenagers. As many scholars note humour is a social and cultural reflection of society.'

'Thank you Rabbi—would you do us the honour of a reading.'

'Indeed I will. Anyone want another bagel before I begin?' The Rabbi clears her throat and reads from a very Jewish, very funny story.

The Eighth Night

The fluffy bagel suit from New York weighed a ton, I thought it would do me, but, as we approached Passover I realised that I would have to diversify. To see a grown man in a fluffy bagel suit once is amusing, to see him wear the same costume repeatedly, meh not so great.

Eventually I found a matzo suit, made from thick cardboard and a tessellated foam coating. Getting through the synagogue door proved to be problematic though, so I stood at the back and left early.

In time I had to rearrange my apartment to accommodate the growing collection; the bagel, matzo, and hamentashen, were in the hallway. The Magen David, and the twenty-two alefbet in the living room and gefilte fish which looked less like an Ashkenazy appetizer and more like an oversized eraser, hung above my bed. Pleasant evenings were spent researching costumes online, hand rinsing giant feet, oversized gloves and a variety of coloured tights.

I enjoyed this new life ; all of the schvitzing beneath the costumes meant I'd dropped a few kilos, I was more confident, happy even. And my standing in the Jewish community was considerable. What had begun three years ago when I moved cities, but was too shy to be part of a new congregation in person, had now grown into a thriving business, where synagogues throughout Melbourne booked me to turn up for high days, holy days and many happy days.

I'd grown accustomed to being privy to private conversations at many events I had attended, as people often forgot that there was a person under the costume. And tonight is no exception. On this the forth night of Channuakh, I hear the Rebbetzin say in hushed tones to that she can tell how much a woman loves her family by the way she cooks her brisket and that she knew a woman who used frozen carrots in their brisket sauce, the women gathered around her tut tut and their mouths curl into contemptuous disbelief.

As the night comes to a close I head out to one of the rooms at the back of the shul to get changed out of my magnificent menorah suit. I don't see the floor because I can't look down and I slip on a jelly donut. How it got there doesn't really matter. Suffice to say that for the first time in my life, I do the splits, to the sound of an almighty rip and a squelch of foam.

I am attempting to rip away the boogie eyes, cherry red lips and a bulbous black sponge of a nose, gasping now for air, when I hear a noise. I peer between the fourth and sixth candle which lay at awkward angles and flash intermittently. A boy around seven or eight runs into the room chasing a spinning dreidel. He takes one look at me, shouts like he is injured, retreats wailing and drops a handful dreidels as he goes.

I see myself as he does, a fifty-something year old man, who has not had a conversation with anyone for years, incandescent with anguish in a battered and probably irreparable, costly menorah suit.

A dreidel skitters across the floor, twirling to a standstill in my face, which is now looming out from a rupture of prolapsed foam. For a moment the words on the dreidel spin as if they are meant just for me. My back spasms as I emerge from the costume, I face the crowd of the curious and concerned congregants.

'Oy!' I sob.

'Vey!' I laugh.

'Nes Gadol Hayah Sham. A great miracle happened here.'

Justine as the Live Dreidel with Rebbetzin Rachel Gutnick

Funny Fellas

'Let's look at the extreme end of using the body for comedic outcomes via US comedian Adrienne Truscott. Here you can see that she is naked from the waist down,' I say, holding up the Doll. 'She is carrying a six-pack of miniature beers. Her show is about rape. She uses her body as an integral part of the show, not hiding or disguising the existence of her body or undermining herself.

'This,' I tell The Group, 'is how Truscott presented herself in her 2013 show, A One-Lady Rape About Comedy Starring Her Pussy and Little Else. The show won the 2013 Edinburgh Foster's Panel-Prize. On the box, you can see the stage setting that Truscott used during her show. There are a variety of framed photos of male stand-up comedians who've either joked about rape or defended the right for comedians to joke about rape. In performing the show naked from the waist down, Truscott was making the point that the female body is, in this instance, the unapologetic object of the show: on view, not derided and not excused. She is also showing that the female body and rape have been the butt of jokes for many male comedians.'

I press the button through the packaging and the Truscott Droll Doll remarks: "I'm doing a show about rape after a long hard week of unequal pay."[40]

Lucy, clearly in awe, says: 'Truscott is so gutsy, she

puts men on notice for making jokes about rape and does it naked from the waist down. Women in comedy have come a long way. I want to give comedy a go. But performing naked as well as being funny, I just don't think I'm up for that.'

I show The Group the Nakkiah Lui Droll Doll. There is an Aboriginal flag printed on the packaging and a description of her hilarious ABC show (now available on iView) Kiki & Kitty. "Kiki & Kitty is about a little black girl in a big white world whose vagina is her best friend."

'When we employ the joke envelope and think about who has been the butt of the joke, namely women, and the use of comedy by the oppressed, Nakkiah turns the joke envelope inside out. As an Aboriginal woman, making a show about her vagina is comedic genius. It turns oppression into power, mocking the dominant ideology of post-colonialism and racism against black people in Australia. As Nakkiah says: "Kiki & Kitty was created as a platform to celebrate sexuality, which in narratives about Aboriginal women tends to be either denied or decried. We're not empowered by our sexuality—so often, when we were growing up, we were told that we weren't clean. A lot of these ideas are used to oppress Aboriginal people: you're dirty, so you get your kids taken away."[41]'

'Lui uses the power of comedy as a political and feminist statement. She is also trail-blazing, forging a path, making representation as a minority in a mainstream medium. And this will encourage others to do the same. When we see ourselves represented, it validates our stories and also it erodes the white male comedic topography.'

'So good,' I say, marvelling at the likeness and the attention to detail on the outfit.

'And this,' I say, taking another Droll Doll from the shelf, 'is the comedian who broke comedy and called out self-deprecation for what it is.'

I hold up the Hannah Gadsby Droll Doll, who comes complete with thick-rimmed spectacles which waggle when she utters a line from her show Nanette: "I have built a career out of self-deprecating humour and I don't want to do that anymore. It's not humility, it's humiliation."[42]

'Have you all seen Nantte?' I ask. The Group nods. 'Then you'll know that the show was a meta-narrative about comedy. Nanette subverted the form of comedy by allowing us to feel another person's pain, not because we are laughing at it, but quite the opposite in fact: because Gadsby was deconstructing it for us. Gadsby leaves the audience with the tension, rather than the relief of the tension through a joke.

'Gadsby tells a funny story but then re-tells it with the truthful ending, not the ending she had previously used to garner laughter. Gadsby doesn't give us the relief that comedy usually gives us, instead they make us question what, in fact, comedy is.

'All of the Droll Dolls erode the male-dominated topography of the comedic landscape and many have changed the nature and purpose of self-deprecation and, in some cases, abandoned it all together. The Droll Doll production line can hardly keep up with the proliferation of female comedians. Women performing in the Melbourne International Comedy Festival in 2015 made up just 19%, but in 2019, according to the Melbourne International Comedy Festival, they made up a staggering 44%.'[43]

I show The Group the rows of Funny Fella Dolls and say: 'The Droll Doll manufacturers wanted to produce only female comics but realised that a collection of Funny Fella Dolls would actually complement the range. As astute businesswomen, they knew that demand for the Funny Fella Dolls would be massive. And they were right.

They have, however, limited the range of Funny Fellas, and a condition of them being stocked in stores is that there must be an equal number of Droll Dolls to Funny Fellas. A great way of calling out the ongoing subtle and not so subtle and pervasive nature of sexism.'

Andrew, who is standing in front of the shelf of Funny Fellas, next to a sign that ITEM WITHDRAWN: 'Oh, they withdrew my favourite comedian, Louis C.K. Too bad he stuffed up, yeh? I love his comedy.'

'Ah yes,' I respond. 'I was actually pleased that the Droll Doll manufacturers withdrew him from the line-up of Funny Fellas.'

'So what happened, what did this Louis guy do?' asks Ruth who, you can tell by the way she's rolling her eyes, doesn't really want to know.

'Well,' I say, 'in late 2017, Louis C.K., whose popularity was comparable to Seinfeld's, was accused of and admitted to taking comedians—women of course—who weren't as successful as him (I mean, really how could they be?) up to his hotel room and without their permission, masturbating in front of them.

'As Eliza Skinner wrote in her article, "Famous Dick Jokes Are Just The Beginning", "the comedy scene is a complex masculine culture of sexism and abuse that has gone unchecked, thus posing a huge barrier for female comedians." Skinner goes on to say: "Should I tell you about the headliner who told my tits I was 'too hot to be funny' before I even said a word? Or about the host at a comedy club who told the audience he'd "love to smell my pussy, after I got on stage?"[44]

'When the revelations about C.K. broke, Melanie Piper wrote; "The lines between fact and fiction in his semi-autobiographical stage and television work thinned and frayed, as the kernel of many of his jokes was made apparent".[45] In other words, if you listened to Louis C.K.'s material, he clearly mined his personal life for material, which many comedians do,' I say.

'To clarify, when talking about Louis C.K. I am using this as an example of humour and power and the abuse of that power in the US comedy scene and whilst that scene will have its specificities, there are similarities between the Australian, UK, and the US comedy circuits. And sometimes when considering examples from places other than our own, this brings to light hidden aspects of our home-grown cultures.

'Does anyone listen to the Marc Maron WTF podcast?' I ask. The Group shakes their heads. 'Well, Marc is a friend of Louis C.K., and on his podcast, post-C.K. revelations, Maron admitted to hearing rumours about Louis but didn't want to believe them. Maron concurred after the revelations that the comedy room environment is: "a damn free-for-all" and that "there is no safe space created for women." He went on to say, "what we really don't know is how much bullshit they have to deal with on top of working out how to get on stage and deal with how to become a comic, on top of that they have to deal with all of us, all of the male bullshit that's what they have to deal with. There's no HR department in comedy, no place to go to have grievances heard."[46]

'Maron's comments make clear what is at stake for aspiring female comedians. There simply is no alternative for women who enter a largely unregulated environment. The comedian Laurie Kilmartin spells out the consequences; "All new comics need the same thing: huge amounts of stage time. There are no shortcuts in stand-up comedy. The quest to become a good comedian is brutal. It takes at least 10 years of performing, almost every night. Female comics do a lot of calculating, finding alternate routes to a career. 'I just won't try to get a spot at that club tonight—he's there.' 'I just won't perform at that club ever—he runs it.' 'I just won't get on that TV show—he books it."[47]

'This reinforces how problematic it is for women to navigate the live stand-up comedy scene and the disparity between opportunities afforded women compared to men.'

'Megh Write says; "Maybe Louis never masturbates in front of an unsuspecting person ever again, but there were soft consequences for this. The entire discussion hinged on when does Louis get to come back? and almost none on, how do we make our scene safer?"[48]

'And while Louis C.K.'s actions were deplorable, the contemporary discourse in response to the accusations shone a spotlight on a world that has long existed without censorship, because it is after all just jokes—right?'

'All you had to do was watch any of his stand-up shows or Netflix series and it was obvious that his material reflected his real life,' Lucy says to Ruth.

'Yes, and while I'm no expert,' Ruth replies, 'doesn't Freud say something like: "humour is an antidote to brutal and hostile behaviour that has been forbidden by law. Telling jokes is seen as a verbal invective to this. What jokes make possible is not the expression of the hostile thought but the expression of a hostile thought that would otherwise be criticised or penalised if expressed openly. The joke endeavours to push criticism out of sight."[49]'

'Indeed,' I reply. 'What is said in the name of humour has long been permitted because it's just jokes. And the comedy room environment, as we will see on the next part of the tour, has permitted behaviour that is seen as being part of the comedy culture, leaving nothing off limits in terms of material or behaviour. This is because comedy rooms have predominantly been occupied by men, in a locker room environment.

'But look timing is everything in comedy.' I check my watch. 'So, I'm afraid we'll have to move on.'

'Aww, humour me, please!' Ruth replies. 'Let me look at the Droll Dolls a while longer, I simply cannot get enough of them.'

'I know,' says Lucy. 'They're just so right on, made by empowered women via a social enterprise, I just love it.' Lucy gets out her phone and takes a photo of herself holding up the Zoe Coombs Marr 'Dave Droll Doll,' She grins and says, 'Straight to my Instagram, #genderandcomedy #funnywomen#prettyfunny.'

'I saw Zoe's show Trigger Warning at the Melbourne International Comedy Festival,' Lucy tells us. 'It was just so funny and so meta, the way she pilloried blokes in the comedy scene. Zoe plays this character called Dave, a parody of hack male comedians that proliferate in comedy rooms. She says she did it as a way of "existing within that space."[50] Coombs takes the mickey out of them while being one of them. It was hilarious, you could see guys squirming in their seats because of how good she was at being a bloke telling bad jokes well.'

'Yes,' I reply, 'Zoe's show is a great example of how women have used what doesn't work in comedy as a tool of defiance. Zoe made fun of the comedy room scene.

Zoe is a gay woman dressed as a man, it was genius. And while she satirised the 'Daves' of the comedy scene, who are often so very gauche and amateur, her show was in fact incredibly polished. It won her loads of awards, and she toured it nationally and internationally. Showing that audiences are receptive to hearing about and recognising the sexism found in the amateur comedy scene. Before we go to the shoe department does anyone need the toilet?'

Shameless

As we ascend the escalator to the shoe department to I tell The Group; 'I grew up in Sunderland North East England, where working men's clubs were a virtual exclusion zone for women performing comedy. It wasn't until 2010 that women were even allowed to be members of working men's clubs in the UK. Until then women could enter clubs only if male members signed them in. Working men's clubs formed an integral part of the community, although this has changed in recent years, in part due to the emergence of alternative venues. In their heyday, though, there were over 4,000 clubs across the UK, mainly in northern working-class areas.[51]

Spracklen says that 'The north is a place where white, working-class masculinity is constructed and performed'. Russell also notes that 'The North has generally been coded as masculine.[52]

I lost my accent not long after arriving in Australia, mainly to stop having to repeat myself but also to rid myself of the shame of being perceived as an uneducated Northerner.

This responds to Bakhtin's idea of the chronotope (1984) to illuminate the way that Northernness is often used to signify a time as well as a place (consider the persistent old fashioned images of flat caps, mills and whippets connected with the North of England).[53] The land of 'Eeh by gum'.

'My point being,' I say, as we step off the escalator into the shoe department, 'Is that voice is an important element in a stand-up comedian's persona. These mixed linguistic registers can be a way to challenge how some stand-up comedians are still trapped within the restrictions of their embodied cultural capital and the effects of a rigid Northern chronotope.[54] Much the way gender restricts access to comedy rooms, so too does voice.

And comedy, like class is about inclusion and exclusion. Comedy can give voice to the voiceless. Doing comedy though means that the comedian must be stay on top, literally in an elevated space on stage, but also linguistically and be victorious. And as we have seen through the Droll Doll collection, self-deprecation is so yesterday and representation in comedy is broadening, beyond the traditional working men's clubs and comedy rooms.

When I started doing comedy it was agonising because the visceral response I felt was one I knew well and that was a feeling of shame. I failed year twelve spectacularly, twice, so I expected to fail forever more. My home environment did not encourage academic aspirations and the wider discourse, (which of course I didn't call it that at the time) was that The North was a place of industry, of working class, of the uneducated and the poor.

Over time that sense of shame eroded and morphed into mettle. Comedy, as we have seen is a take charge artform, where the very point of it is to be seen and heard.

The function of comedy is to illicit laughter as a result of our shortcomings and our perspective on the world. It took some time to master the art of comedy and to come out on top, to gain agency, feel empowered and to occupy spaces where we have not previously been allowed.

So accent is often something we lose in order to fit in and accent is often something we put on to elevate our status, and accent is an integral part of where we can and cannot gain access too.

'So,' I wink knowingly at The Group, as we stand amongst the impossibly high heels and non-threatening footwear, which is ostensibly made for those working in the non-profit sector.

'Let me rip forth in my best Northern dialect, with a story that flips the Bakhtin paradigm that women are the locus of so many unpleasant fluids. Sit down, try on some shoes and enjoy this tale of agency in a time of adversity.'

Spit and Polish

Uncle John comes in for the kiss. He smells of Germolene. His head, shoes and nails are as shiny as the one-pound coin he's holding up high, like it's a golden doubloon just in from a shipwreck. It's the last Friday of school term, before we finish up for the long summer that is never hot. We've just finished lunch, a pasty from Marks & Spencer, dead posh.

Uncle John never just hands over the pound coin, so I can

say 'thank you', then head back down to school. Instead, he holds it in the air, the wiry red hair across his hand tufty, his nails short and even.

My nails are stubby, and the cuticles are ragged and misshapen. My mam tells me that I should push the cuticles down or my nails won't be able to breathe properly. I think she's daft for saying that, though, because I know that nails can't suffocate.

When he comes in for the kiss, saying 'Here's your pocket money then, Elsie,' his beady eyes are blinking, the hairs sprouting out of his nostrils seem to bristle like there are lots more in there wanting to push their way out, and he smells like cleaning fluids.

I don't want to smell like cleaning fluid, but I want to feel clean. I've only got one school shirt and my school skirt is too long. If I try to shorten it, by rolling it over and over at the waist, like the other girls do, it just looks like a badly cut piece of cardboard, not sassy like theirs. I've just turned fourteen, and my body is lumping and bumping and sprouting out all over and I've begun to smell strange and sour. I have a bath once a week but that's after my stepdad's been in it. I've seen adverts on telly for Radox bubble bath. The water's blue and the bubbles are white and fluffy as candy floss. I'd love a bath like that.

When Uncle John, glistening and odorous, comes in for the kiss, it doesn't matter what shape I make my mouth or what angle I put my head on. It happens every time. As his lips touch mine, a big bit of his spit spurts into my mouth. It's acrid and cold for a very short moment, then warm as it swishes around my mouth.

He used to just give me a bag of kets: taffees, chocolate bars, fizzy chews and pink musk sticks. I hate musk sticks: they smell of old ladies and I only eat them when there's nothing else left. Once, a filling fell out after I'd eaten a slab of taffee, so my mam told Uncle John that he wasn't to give me kets anymore. That's when he started giving me a pound coin instead. When there were kets, he'd just hand them over. That was that, the plastic bag heavy and full. But getting the money changed everything.

On this Friday, the last one before the end of the year, I sit fidgeting at the table, waiting for the moment to tell my news. I wait for the roller brush to move backwards and forwards over the Axminster, catching up all the crumbs from the pasties. It's a real trick to eat without flaking the pastry onto the floor. I can't do it. Aunt Monica can't do it either. She's forever brushing crumbs off her pinny onto the floor, saying, 'I'll get on to them after I've had me lunch.' Uncle John can eat without dropping crumbs, though sometimes there are tiny flecks that stay stuck to his lips, and sometimes those flecks end up in my mouth after the kiss.

I go to Aunt Monica's for lunch because she lives close to school. It's handy and it saves my mam the lunch money. I'd rather be with my friends, though, lining up for whatever is being served and chatting while we wait. The whole of the bottom part of the school is taken up serving school lunches, so in the afternoon, the classrooms smell of cabbage and chips. Sometimes the smell is so bad, even if it's freezing outside, we have to open the windows so that we can breathe properly.

Other schools have canteens and nicer uniforms than us. Our blazers are brown and we get called 'Shit Backs,' by other schools. Sometimes on the way to or from Aunt Monica's, kids yell out, 'Shit back, shit back, shit back,' in singsong. I don't tell Aunt Monica that I get called a 'Shit Back,' because I'm not allowed to say 'shit' in the house.

I tell Aunt Monica other things though, like the shoes I want from Timpson's; they have a wedge heel, are a deep blue velvety colour and are reet cushty.

Stacy Johnson has a pair. I like Stacy, but I hate her as well because of her perm and her house, which has central heating. We've got a Calor gas heater, which only warms up a very small spot in the house. Our cat Tibby sits so close to the heater that he has a permanent brown scorch mark on his grey fur.

When I tell Aunt Monica about the things I want, she always says that she'll pray for me on Sunday. Aunt Monica only prays on a Sunday, because she's very busy the rest of the time, making lunches and dinners and going into town on the bus to do the shopping. Aunt Monica hasn't got any children. Sometimes when she's giving me a butter mint from the jar after my lunch, her eyes go misty and she says, 'I wish you were mine, pet.'

I always feel a bit sad when she says that. Aunt Monica lives in the house she grew up in with her brother, Uncle John. They spoil me with kets and pocket money, I suppose, because they don't have children of their own. I do like the thought of sitting next to Aunt Monica watching telly at night, getting a butter mint out of the jar whenever I fancy one, but I'd miss my mam, so maybe it's for the best. And besides, my hair's thick and black and Aunt Monica's is very white and straight, so people would always know that I wasn't really hers.

The days of the week match the meal at Aunt Monica's. There's panacalty on a Monday, made quickly because Aunty Monica does the washing on a Monday, which takes all day and leaves the house smelling like a wet dog. Once, Aunt Monica put black pudding into the panacalty. Parts of it were was soft and spongy. Other bits were firm and gristly. Usually I can chat all through lunch, about what teacher we've had that morning, or about how many times and who Mr Hill gave the cane that day, or about how hard algebra is. But on the black pudding day, I don't say a word, because I'm worried it might rise out of my throat and spew all over the tablecloth.

Tuesdays are a stringy corned-beef sandwich, with butter as thick as the bread. On Wednesdays, the egg and chips look like they are having a swim in the oil that laps around the edges of the plate. We have sports on a Wednesday and the pressure of the pudding after we have the egg and chips always slows me down to a crawl. The pudding alternates between spotted dick and jam roly-poly. I've not seen a chart or anything, but Aunt Monica always knows which week is which for the pudding. The pudding is made from suet. It swells as it cooks, and it keeps swelling in your tummy hours after you've eaten it.

How the suet can swell so much is just another of the list of mysteries at Aunt Monica's. Like why Aunt Monica has never married and why there is always a pile of old copies of the Radio

Times on the pantry shelf. And the ultimate mystery: the tiny bottle of Holy Water from Lourdes, that sits on the mantel piece next to the picture of Mary. Aunt Monica says that even a tiny drop of Holy Water has healing powers, but when I had a bad cut from falling over once, I asked if I could splash some of it on the cut. Aunt Monica had looked at me like I was a radge and had said 'Absolutely not.'

On Thursdays, Aunt Monica puts on a bit of orange lipstick, takes out her rollers and dabs Lily of the Valley perfume behind her ears. Then she goes on the bus into town for her shopping: pasties and butter mints from Marks & Spencer, meat and vegetables from Jackie White's market and for two weeks in summer, she buys strawberries from Binns. When she serves the strawberries, Aunt Monica never asks if I want sugar and carnation milk on them. She just serves them with both and says, 'You can tell it's summer now, mind.'

Thursday's lunch is a floury bap with a bit of hard cheese inside and three slices of salted tomatoes on the edge of the plate. There's that much salt on the tomatoes, it looks like a snow-cap melting. I'd rather not have the salt on the tomatoes, but that's how they're served. I always like Friday's lunch best: a pasty and a nice cup of tea.

This Friday is even better than normal because I've got my news to tell. When Aunt Monica finally puts away the roller brush from the crumb-gathering and we take the white tablecloth outside to shake it out, my belly does a little flip of excitement.

The wind makes the outside toilet door bang a bit and

Aunt Monica's pinny flaps like a mad bird as we step out into the backyard. Me and Aunt Monica each take a corner of the tablecloth, step away from each other, do three quick shakes and watch the last pasty crumbs go flying into the air like dandruff. We fold the cloth from left to right, and then laugh as we shimmy towards each other. As the tips of Aunt Monica's fingers touch mine, I tell her my news.

'I've got a summer job, Aunt Monica, at Chalkie's fruit shop. It's just one day a week, but he's going to give me nine pounds.'

My heart is pumping and I am flushed with the joy of telling her. She hugs me, crumpling up the tablecloth between us. 'Pet,' she says, 'pet, that's just grand, that is. I've been praying for you to get all of the things you want and now you can.'

We go back inside. From her apron, Aunt Monica pulls out a butter mint, touches the side of my cheek, and says, 'You're growing up fast now, pet.'

As she begins to clatter the dishes against the metal sink, she shouts out to Uncle John, who I know is waiting for me at the front door: 'John, the bairn has some news.'

He raises the gold coin as he sees me walking towards him. 'Here's your pocket money then, Elsie.'

I hear Aunt Monica doing the dishes, humming a tune. He leans towards me, blocking the doorway. I hold my breath and his gaze and spurt it out:

'I've got a summer job, so I don't need the coins anymore. Thanks, though, Uncle John.'

His mouth hangs and his neck is straining. A large globule of spit spills from his drooping lips right onto the tip of one of his brown shiny shoes. He's standing in the doorframe, still as a statue, as I duck under his raised arm and head out into that last Friday of term. Leaving Uncle John to his spit and polish.

The Book Store

'Ok,' I say to The Group as we exit the department store, 'whilst there is an abundance of research and analysis carried out on successful comedians, there are few studies examining where it all begins. So let's head to the comedy room, which—for many—is the first place they give stand-up comedy a go. For this part of the C.O.M.E.D.Y. Tour, I'll wave the HA! HA! flag a bit more to create frivolity, because although we are going to a comedy room and these places are often the antithesis of fun.'

We move through the mall and I tell The Group: 'When I first started doing comedy over fifteen years ago, what I encountered, on the whole, were hostile places. I was often the only woman on the line-up, and it would at times take me months to get a spot in a room. Rooms were run by men and booked mainly men, creating a gatekeeper environment. When I performed, I felt the content of my material about working in the non-profit sector and being a parent and a woman was an anomaly amongst the dominant voices of young men, who talked mainly about being single, masturbating and eating MacDonald's at 2am. There were many times when I was 'thrown under the bus' by the MC, who either dismissed my material or announced me in a way that was derogatory, misogynistic or anti-Semitic. Remaining in the comedy scene was gruelling. In time, I created opportunities to perform comedy away from rooms. On many occasions, I vowed not to return to rooms, because I found the experience counterproductive to being funny.

'Happy to let you know though, that the increase in the number of women on the comedy scene has meant that there are now formal and informal networks of women in comedy. There are rooms run by women. There's Funny Women, a global platform creating opportunities for women in comedy, Facebook groups and in comedy rooms there are women supporting other women. So women can perform without being subject to censorship and or comparison to male comedians. But in those early days, comedy was a gruelling enterprise. At the time too my then husband was perplexed by weekly sojourns into comedy rooms and confronted by my growing appetite for more than just five-minute spots. He advised me very early on that I wasn't funny and that I should be prepared for the audience to throw bricks at me. To my credit I retorted: "Means we might finally get the renovation done."'

'Go you!' Ruth retorts enthusiastically.

I smile back at Ruth. 'The thing is, the more material I wrote, the more I wanted to perform. I just never felt sated and I never felt I was getting any better. I was on the scene once a week and although I went on to do comedy festivals and fringe shows, essentially I fitted my new hobby into the family's timetable. I really wanted to do comedy full time, I just didn't have the gumption.

'The hostility I and many other women experienced in

comedy rooms is not limited to Melbourne, as we heard with the C.K. incident and in Northern UK. As Lindy West aptly comments, "comedy has long fetishized itself on not being censored and the environment in which it is performed in isn't censored."[55] West cites an incident in a bar where a woman heckles a comedian who has told a rape 'joke'. The comedian responds by telling the audience how funny it would be if the woman was raped by all of the men in the room.[56] This indicates to the heckler, a woman, that she has been put on notice and that she is not welcome in the room, nor can she assume that she will be safe in the room or when she leaves. West cites the incident as an example of the ongoing gendered violence directed at women in the guise of a 'joke'. West says, "this is not humour, but a form of 'accepted' misogyny, and a mechanism of silencing women and keeping them at home and hidden."[57]

'When I read that line in Lindy's book something in me shifted. I understood finally that it wasn't just about my perception of not being funny enough, it was the environment I was working in that was the problem. I wondered too why this is talked about in academic circles, the idea of gender and comedy, but why wasn't this mainstream, why aren't there more books written about it.'

It's dusk now, and the sun is setting in the west on this quiet Monday night in Melbourne.

'Let's duck into this bookstore.' I guide The Group into the tranquil space, timber bookshelves bedecked with a splendour of spines, potted palms adding to the cultivated aura. White orbs of pendant lighting glow above the classifications: Crime Thriller, Australian Literature, Poetry, an embarrassment of self-help books, (an embarrassment being the collective noun of self-help books).

'Anything on comedy?' I ask. The young person at the counter peers at their computer.

'We've got some lovely lined journals to write in that have funny titles.

'*My herpes outbreak tracker*. Or a joke journal you can write your jokes in, or how about a Seth Rogen colouring in book?'

'Hmm, not quite what I was after. Do you have a specific section on humour perhaps or stand-up comedy?' I respond.

'Computer says no. But we do have *The Joke* by Milan Kundera and *Dante's Divine Comedy Inferno.*'

'It would seem our collective wisdom on humour is yet to be written in the pages of blank journals,' I respond despondently.

'Sorry, we just don't get much in the way of books on comedy or humour in general really, is there anything else I can help you with?'

'Maybe. Would you be able to make room on the shelf for when the C.O.M.E.D.Y. Tour is published? And if possible shine a light on it, even one of those clip-on book torches would be fine..'

She laughs, 'Sure that would be doable.'

The Group are leafing through novels and considering the manager's weekly list of favourites.

'It's curious isn't it that there is so little written about comedy, especially about amateur stand-up comedy.' I interrupt their browsing.

'Perhaps it's hard to write about or it just has to be done and not deconstructed.' Proffers Andrew.

'Absolutely,' I reply, 'as soon as you deconstruct comedy it stops being funny. There are funny books, laugh out loud short story collections like Kevin Barry's' *'That Old Country Music.'* or books that bring us infinite joy and pleasure. But it would be great to liberate comedy from the confines of the comedy room and create a literary masterpiece on stand-up comedy.'

'A comedy bible of sorts?' Questions Lucy.

'Yes, like Grossman does it in *A Horse Walks into a Bar,*[58] and Lindy West deconstructs the hostility of the comedy room beautifully in Shrill[59] and of course Melbourne's own Joanne Brookfield's book No Apologies[60] is nothing short of magnificent. But for the general public, those who want to give comedy a go, are curious about humour, it's function and exquisite complexity, it would seem you just can't just walk into a bookstore and be shown the section on humour. It's confounding to me really.'

'Oh Look,' I segue, 'they've got back copies of the Writer's Victoria quarterly publication. Oh my, this one from way back has a story I wrote about those excruciating days of early motherhood. Can I read it to you? It was when

I had just started doing comedy and I was using comedy as a way to bring light into the monotony. I actually don't know how I would have got through those early years without comedy.'

I read the story as The Group take a seat in the comfort of well-worn leather armchairs:

Price Check

Josie pulls on her jeans, three red leather bangles and a shirt that can be unbuttoned modestly.

There's a slightly sour smell in the air. The washing spills out of the laundry basket. She pulls back the covers on the bed. As she draws back the blind, dust motes rise like ghosts in the strong morning light.

Three-and-a-half hours, at least. She knows that she shouldn't count but adding up the hours of sleep helps her feel like she has some control over the night that has passed.

From the other end of the house, the spoon is reaching its crescendo as he stirs his coffee. Her jaw is clenched in irritation. She gathers the plastic bag, full of wipes, pooey nappies and an empty tin of ointment from the change table. Glancing in the mirror on her way out, she sees her hair is in fuzzy disarray. She pushes it down with her free hand.

'See you later—have a good one.' A last slurp of coffee, a crunch of toast, one perfunctory kiss, and he is gone.

She watches his broad back recede down the quiet street,

where the sun is just starting to climb. Milk from her engorged breasts begins to leak through her shirt as she stands in the front yard. The garden has the classic rented look: slightly desolate, in need of a mow, and all the charm of a cup of tea gone cold.

Back inside, she positions the cushions, brings the infant to her, her right hand supporting his head, the left cradling his body. She feels a tingling light-headedness, followed by a sense of relief as the milk drains out of her. The baby belches, leaving a thin sour stream on her sleeve.

Stay calm and relax. Some people say chocolate is not food, it's just chocolate. No husband has ever been shot while doing the dishes.

She arranges the fridge magnets one more time. It seems like she is always there in the house, always just being there with the baby.

The radiant heat from the traffic and the concrete throbs. It's 10am and already over 30 degrees. If she closes her eyes, she can pretend that the roaring noise is the ocean, not the traffic. The northern suburbs of Melbourne are heavy and tired from the incessant heat.

It took her until now, until she had the baby, to understand the seasons and to understand how the sun travelled across the sky in Australia.

Arriving from the UK ten years before, understanding those things hadn't mattered. That was a time in her life when she hardly understood herself, never mind her surroundings.

When she was pregnant, someone had said Oh how lovely

you're having a Spring baby. It clicked, then, that Spring was late in the year, that the heat came at Christmas time, that an English winter was an Australian summer. She had not understood it till she had birthed, nor had she ever before looked at or cared about the direction the sun travelled during the day.

The position of the pram could be changed to suit the direction of the sun. The sun rose in the east, travelled north, and finally set in the west. It mattered somehow that she knew where the sun would be, so she could change the direction of the pram as she walked around the streets.

Milk, nappies, coffee, something for dinner the list was created to put purpose into her day. Unlike the blur of feeding, the thin streams of vomit always across her clothes, and the interminable stretch of the day.

She knows no one in the suburb where she lives. Most days she speaks only to the check-out chicks at the supermarket. Often, she stares at passers-by, wishing that they would be her friends.

She pauses on her walk and looks up. Nothing assails her quite like the silvery green of gum trees, the endless varieties, the red explosion of colour, their gracefulness, their starkness. It always makes her stop, heightens her sense of loneliness. Reminds her that she is now in the Southern Hemisphere. Australia.

The baby sleeps through the walk down to the supermarket. She usually has an hour or so before her breasts spring a leak, before she must unharness herself, find somewhere to sit and feed the infant. Then she can release the engorged heaviness into the infant's wide, hungry mouth.

She passes the black and brown Alsatian, barking at number 365. The renovation that seems to be taking forever at 451. The garden at 517, made up of a manicured lawn and topiaries in the shape of strange animals with plastic black-and-white stuck-on eyes. It would take hours and hours of work to keep the strange beasts in shape, but she has never seen anyone tend the garden. She imagines that they conduct their topiary work under the cover of darkness, a torch guiding the hedge trimmer, the light deranged and the shadows short.

She crosses the road to the supermarket; the heat seems to intensify around all the parked cars. The cool air is a blast as she enters. Her shirt is sticking to her back. In the stark bright light, she feels stale.

Her anonymity is amplified by the uniformity of the place, The Grouping of cleaning fluids and toilet paper, frozen items and boxes of cereals, an orderly flow of people in and out, the shelves always stacked, the shelf stackers never seen.

She contemplates the slithered tuna enrobed in a succulent mornay, surrounded by a trio of spring vegetables and wonders if it really is food fit for humans or, as the tin suggests, for animal consumption only. She trawls up and down the supermarket, holding a pacifier in her hand, momentarily dreaming that this could be the answer to the endless sleepless nights, then hangs it back on its hook knowing that her choice to breastfeed means that she is the eternal pacifier. The very thought of it makes her nipples tingle, and not in a pleasurable way.

Haribo Gold Bears $3.30 each WAS $4.40 SAVE $1.10 25% OFF. Haribo Gold Bears Mini.1 Pack 250g. Some lines for the bar code. Some numbers beneath the bar code. The number 22 in a circle.

She places the yellow and green sign for Haribo Gold bears into the basket underneath the pram, pays for the food that she has bought for dinner, the nappies, the coffee, and leaves the supermarket.

The heat hits her like a heavy sponge. She begins to walk up the hill back home and feels something beyond the usual drag of tiredness. She stops momentarily to understand what the feeling is, and places it: it is the feeling of excitement tinged with purpose.

Between the feeds, the burping and the pooey nappies that night, she sits by the glow of her computer. Her tiredness makes her sway and almost hallucinate, but she keeps going. Haribo Gold bears $2.20 each WAS $4.40 SAVE $2.10. The slightest change.

The next day she goes down the hill, purposeful, the drone of domesticity a momentary backdrop. She enters the supermarket.

Haribo Gold bears $2.20 each WAS $4.40 SAVE $2.10. She places the label onto the shelf. She does her shopping, slowly: bread, eggs, baby wipes, washing-up liquid, some fruit and a small box of tea. She slows her pace down, dawdling, not caring that her time might run out, that her breasts may spring a leak, or even spurt. Eventually she realizes that it won't happen today, that today she will have to go home without seeing her *work in action, that the warmth spreading across her shirt and the baby's stirring movements means that she must leave, now, before the infant begins to bawl.*

When she gets home, her shirt is damp, with map-like patterns running across it. The souring milk smell makes her almost dry retch. The infant's hands are clenched, his face is red from crying. She feeds the baby calming him with a slight rocking movement. She changes out of her soggy shirt, places the infant into the bassinet—the one that can be wheeled around the house—and places it next to her computer.

In the first week, there was an orange string bag of onions. 1 kilo WAS $2.50 SAVE $1.00, imported cherries from the US, an assortment of confectionary, pet food and an electrical juicing machine, all altered slightly. It took until Thursday, four days into the alterations, for her to be in the store to hear it:

'Price check. Price check on grocery.'

She listens, pretending to be fascinated in a show-and-tell magazine. A film star's ex-lover is now married to her best friend. Another film star reveals her fat-busting techniques. She peers over the magazine as the customer says: 'The sign said $4.00, it says it's on special.'

She watches the young assistant go up aisle seven to bring back the yellow and green sign. The numbers slightly altered, the lines changed. Her sign, oh-so-carefully mimicked, oh-so-carefully changed on her computer. Her almost-forgotten training as a graphic designer, dulled by the exhausting birth, the endless feeding, the intense boredom of early motherhood, sparking strangely back into the life because of a packet of Haribo Gold bears.

The checkout chick shakes her head as the scanner waves over the top. She shakes her head again after several futile attempts, waiting for the expected beep sound. The customer shows signs of irritation, eyes moving slightly upwards, a short sigh, a shuffle of the shoulders, a pursing of the lips, a quick glance at her mobile phone.

The Haribo Gold bears are given to the customer at the price displayed on the yellow and green label.

It was small things at first, then large packets of toilet paper, gourmet ice-cream crazily priced at $12.00 boasting pistachios, drizzles of salted-caramel and shards of toffee. WAS $12.00 NOW $2.00. Her head is dull with sleeplessness, her 'work' interrupted by the shrill cry of the infant wanting another feed.

A month in, and her living room is strewn with supermarket labels. Her walks up and down the hill to the supermarket have become a daily thrill. She cannot know who will buy what when she is there. She can only hope.

Forty-two days in and as she enters the supermarket, she feels dull and lugubrious, the incessant ache of her nearly full breasts, the buzz of tiredness making her temples throb.

The saxophone crescendo to Jerry Rafferty's Baker Street filters through as she approaches the nappy aisle. She begins to hum along to the lyrics.

Through the song's rhythm another sound comes to her. The sound of alchemy at work, the moment she has till now, only imagined.

There has been one call, then in quick succession another. She hurries down the aisle, not even bothering to get the nappies that she has come in for.

There is another call and another. She stands in the bright light and smiles; her backdrop displaying signs boasting that everything is Special.

All five checkouts in operation, are all making the same call. Along with the call, she sees the flashing lights indicating that the operator is requesting assistance. They are like beacons. Then, the noise, such a beautiful melody.

Five checkout chicks yell at once: 'Price check, price check, price check, price check, price check.'

'Ha!' says Ruth, 'I remember those days well, the interminable boredom of early motherhood, I baked a lot in those days just to be able to start and finish something in one day and feel a vague sense of accomplishment.'

I smile back at her. 'Let us continue.'

The Comedy Room

I lead The Group through a graffitied laneway in downtown Melbourne and take them through a doorway that could easily be missed. As we ascend a stone stairway, concave in parts and worn down from all of the male comedians traipsing up and down them week after week, I say: ''Learning to be a comedian is like learning any other set of performance skills. It's not a question of having a mystical ability to be funny: it's a question of acquiring techniques. Actors have developed a vast range of techniques over decades and they also have a kind of folkloric existence: No such repertoire of activities exists to train potential stand-up comedians.'[61] 'A new comic is required to establish a relationship with the audience, which makes them believe that he or she is funny.'[62] For many amateur comedians, their first gig may be the only time that they have stood in front of a live audience and used a microphone. And just as Simone De Beauvoir says, 'One is not born a woman, but rather becomes one.'[63] Likewise, one is not born a comedian, rather one becomes one.

'This,' I tell The Group, gesturing to the space we are standing in, 'is a typical comedy room. Note the dim lighting, the assortment of mismatched chairs, the sticky carpet and the disproportionate number of men to women. 'Hell is not a divine comedy, it's an open mic night, and open mic nights are essential to the development of an aspiring comedian and at the same time are problematic spaces.'[64]

'Comedy is generally performed in licensed venues, not just legally under the Public Halls and Liquor Licencing Acts, but culturally as places for comic transgression.'[65] And because comedy rooms are located in bars in licensed venues, with the inevitable mix of alcohol and a lack of industry standards, this often means that women's experiences of performing stand-up comedy differs from men's experience.

'Nights in comedy rooms begin at around seven or eight in the evening and often run until ten or eleven pm. There's rarely any remuneration to perform, not even a beer, and the time commitment just to perform a five-minute set is considerable. Rooms are run in a variety of ways; some are sign-up nights where a comedian turns up, puts their name down and waits their turn to do a five-minute set, some you can book a spot. Rooms are predominantly run by men who, it would seem, prefer to book men.

'Brookfield claims that because 'comedy rooms are dominated by men, not only does that lay the foundations for the culture of the room and who can get in, but also what is said on stage is so skewed towards a male perspective that it skews what comedy actually is.'[67] 'So that when a woman does get on the bill— and for a long time there has often only been one woman on the bill—her lone voice comes to represent all women. So the essence of what happens in a comedy room is an issue of power—where it resides and how it is negotiated.'[68]

'I did a gig in a bar one time,' I tell The Group. 'I told a joke about the Aldi Supermarket, how you go in expecting to buy apples, oranges and bananas, but come out with extendable garden shears, a whipper snipper and a gluten extractor. I live in Brunswick and there's no gluten allowed in Brunswick. And then when you get to the end of the long conveyor belt and all of the shopping is hurtling towards you, with only a tiny amount of room to pack your shopping, it's a terrifying experience. The MC back-announced me with this: 'You'd think that Germans would get the length of the conveyor belt right, wouldn't you? After all they built the gas chambers.' The MC knew that I was Jewish, but I didn't call it out, as it felt oddly churlish to do so. But this idle talk is, as Lindy West says, 'the sniggers behind closed doors that fuel the greater fire of men in white hoods and stranger rapes in dark alleys.'[68]

'Before the comedy begins, feel free to go to the bar, get a drink,' I tell them. There are a couple of specials on offer as part of the C.O.M.E.D.Y. Tour, including the *No Apologies Spritzer*, and the *Wry Martini,* a great antidote for the disheartened woman in comedy, the olive is speared with barbed wit.'

When The Group sits back down, I tell them: 'As part

of the preparation for the C.O.M.E.D.Y. Tour, I didn't want to just quote academic references and share my perspective, so I interviewed three female comedians about their experiences on the Melbourne comedy scene. Over the years, I've had numerous informal conversations and have been part of online forums and discussions about being a woman in comedy. Before the 'comedy' begins, I want to share with you these interviews. For the purposes of the C.O.M.E.D.Y. Tour, names have been omitted and voices have been changed.'[69]

I press play on my phone. A pixelated head shot appears with the words 'Comedian with three years of experience' underneath. The altered voice says: *I have worked for a long time with victims of domestic violence. I just started working with perpetrators. I felt safer in a room full of perpetrators than I did in a comedy room line-up, which probably says something actually about what it is to do comedy in a comedy room.*

'When was this recorded?' Andrew asks.

'In 2018,' I reply.

'It just doesn't seem possible,' Andrew says.

I press the next recording, also from a comedian with three years' experience: *The comedian before me told a 'joke' about hunting down women with a cat trap. He couldn't guarantee a squeal of delight but he could guarantee a squeal. I got up on stage and said that the joke made me feel unsafe and violated. The MC responds with 'And that's why women aren't funny'.*

And the next one, from a comedian with over ten years'

experience: *You gig where you want to, and you gig where you feel safe. I refuse to set foot in the Comics Lounge because of the way that they treat women and I advocate for people to do the same, that's a horrific place and, you know, if I had the chance, I'd burn it to the ground.*

And yet another one, this one based on five years' experience: *Many gigs run very late and that means that I'm often doing supermarket shopping late at night after a gig. Many women are, of course, primary caregivers, so before they have left the house, they have a number of domestic tasks to fulfil. And I know some women who gig and have never been to a licensed venue before on their own, for cultural reasons, and they didn't know that they could go into a bar and not have to buy a drink.*

The Group looks perturbed.

The MC, a male about 26 years old, takes the mic off the stand and looks out at the audience, made up of mainly male comedians, and asks: 'Are youse ready for a night of great comedy?'

At 10:45pm, The Group come out of the comedy room looking weary.

'The night went on forever,' Lucy says.

'There was so much racism,' Ruth exclaims.

'One comedian did a rape joke,' Andrew comments.

'One or two were okay. Not hilarious, but okay,' Lucy murmurs.

'And the line-up,' I say, 'was a fairly typical sign-up night with fourteen men and two women on the bill. It's a hostile and prohibitive environment for many to gain a foothold on the comedy scene and then to remain in it and keep performing and perfecting the craft. It takes pure mettle. And what we saw tonight is repeated in many rooms throughout Melbourne.' I say.

'For me there are so few beautiful moments in comedy rooms, for me mainly it is a grind. Occasionally though something happens, a joke I have been working on for weeks begins to work, or I see someone with a real talent who respects and hones their craft, they appear in-between the grim tirade as accidental glitter.'

Accidental Glitter

The shock of it.

The police at Mary's door.

'Can we come in?'

'We're sorry to tell you.'

'Is there someone we can call for you?'

The funeral.

The numbness.

The appalling abyss of despair.

Waking up each morning from a sedative-induced sleep, Corry still gone.

It didn't just happen, Mary had whispered to the police, to the coroner, to Corry's friends.

It didn't just happen, something made her do it.

* * *

This week, Mary goes west. The club's doorway is filled with a huddle of them, waiting for the night to begin, smoking cigarettes and swapping stories.

Inside, she's greeted by the dank smell of smoke and the dregs of beer that have soaked into the carpet over the years. It's the usual kind of set-up: dim lighting, mismatched chairs, an old sofa to one side and a mic on a stand on a make-shift stage.

Kevin, the organiser, is strutting. People come over to him, all of them speaking just a little too loud, wanting to be noticed, needing to know where they have been placed on the line-up.

Kevin takes the mic off the stand and shouts into it: 'Youse all know me, I'm Kevin. How youse all going? Youse ready for big night of laughs, then? So, I'm single, right. I'm single and the other day when I was having a wank, I noticed that my laptop was a bit wet.' There are titters from the audience. Kevin goes on to describe the McDonald's that he had last night and makes a reference to Deliveroo. He finishes with a description of the tomato sauce spurting out of the burger onto his laptop, like cum.

'Let's get our first act up, then, shall we? He's a good friend of mine, a very funny bloke. Let's get him up here—Darren Smith.'

Darren is wearing a beanie, sports a straggly beard and shuffles from side to side. He peers at the top of his hand where he has scrawled some words as prompts. 'Australia's fucked, right? Just look at the way we have to go to prison if we rape a chick. The thing about raping a woman is, that if she's wearing a short skirt she wants it, if she's not wearing a short skirt she's still asking for it because she wants you to be reminded that she's a slut anyway.'

The material circles around the same theme: that he doesn't want to go to prison for raping a woman, but at the same time he doesn't want to stop thinking about how good it would be to screw someone. He ends on a line about using a rape drug so he would never get found out.

Mary sips her water and turns to the next page in her spiral-bound notepad. In the middle column, she makes a note of Darren's name under the heading 'Misogynist' at the bottom of an already long list.

Six more men get up and shout at the audience. One after the other, they tell their 'jokes': they talk about the size of their dicks, their girlfriends and intimate details of their sex lives and their sisters who they hate because they are lesbians. One wants to go back in time and meet Hitler to ask why he couldn't kill all the Jews. They cheer each other on and slap each other on the back as they get on and off the stage.

Mary feels the bile rise as she always does in these places, quietened only because she is there for Corry, because Corry came to these places and tried so hard to do comedy and to understand why it wasn't working for her when it seemed to work so well for the others, for the men.

The chatter she hears during the break is almost as bad as what's said onstage. But she stays. She has her book and the names to chronicle. The festival is only weeks away and she wants to be ready.

Behind her, a tall gangly man called Tim is talking to Kevin about a 'top gig' he did last week, out Moorabbin way. Kevin says he knows the room and is doing a gig there tomorrow. At the bar, Paul swills another beer. He regales the barmaid with a story about his son who is still at school but a 'lazy cunt'. The barmaid keeps herself busy, serving drinks, restocking the fridge. She doesn't engage, and eventually Paul turns away, swigging his beer, talking over the others at the bar instead.

A short stocky man wearing glasses and a cap on backwards walks in and there is a noticeable change in the mood of the room. He's on telly and is doing a spot at the end of the night. He ignores everyone in the room except for Kevin who fawns over him.

'Simon, mate, thanks a lot, good of you to come, mate. We've had a ripper first bracket and we'll get you up after this next lot. Got some sheila who wants to get up, then two more, then you.'

Simon shrugs in response, declines a drink from Kevin and waits at the back of the room.

Mary watches as Paul ambles over to Simon. 'Saw you at the Comic's Lounge last week. Stellar job, mate, stellar. I'm emceeing there next week. How's that Chrissy on the telly there the other night, eh? Did you want to slap her when she asked you not to speak over the top of her?' Simon nods then looks away. Paul stands for a moment, checks his phone, gets another beer, and sits at the front of the room.

Kevin's back on stage, holding a pint in one hand and gripping the mic stand in the other, like he might fall over if he loosens his grasp. 'Youse all have a good break? Do a piss? Have a snort?'

Mary feels tired. She straightens her back, then pulls her cardigan around herself.

'We've got a very special guest on tonight: Simon Worth, from Channel Ten's The Blueprint. Woo!' Kevin lifts his hand and the audience echoes 'Woo!' in response.

'Before Simon comes up, though, we've got the very pretty Suzie.'

A young woman, a little older than Corry, grins to her friend before getting onstage. Kevin tries to kiss her cheek as she walks towards the mic, but Suzie sticks out her hand instead. They duck and weave, and neither shake hands nor kiss. Kevin grimaces, thrusts the mic at her and goes off stage. Suzie, meanwhile, has apparently shaken off the awkward encounter and bounces around onstage. She has curly hair, large glasses and is wearing an oversized cardigan, making her look like a caricature.

Mary feels a wrench in her stomach, whispers 'Corry' to herself, and makes a note in her book: 'one to eight ratio of women to men'. This comment has been written several times with different dates next to it.

'When I started doing comedy, I told my mum, who's a bit deaf, that I wanted to become a comedian.' Suzie has a slight twang to her accent, not quite American, but almost. 'My mum said, can you change colours, can you? I didn't know what she was talking about. Mum, I said to her, I don't have to change colours, I just have to make people laugh. But Suzie, my mum

said, if you want to be a chameleon, you'll have to learn how to change colours.' The woman who Suzie came in with laughs. There are faint titters from the audience. The other comedians are silent. Mary absorbs their silence like a personal affront.

'When I was a kid, I always wanted to play dress-ups and be a princess, then I realised that I hated princesses because their life was only complete once a prince came along. So, then I decided that I wanted to become a unicorn. Because let's face it what's not to like about being able to do a rainbow coloured pooh?' Mary wishes that she had watched Corry do stand-up. Corry had always said, Wait till I get better, Mum. 'To date I've only managed a rainbow hurl, and while it's not attractive, it does indicate my ability to cover vast distances using my stomach muscles alone. And unicorns are cool right? And smart. For a mythical creature, they sure do have a lot of merchandise, so one of them must be getting the royalties somewhere.' At the end of the set, Kevin takes the mic from Suzie and by way of a nod, dismisses her.

'The next guy is a very good friend of mine,' he says.

Mary zones out as the next guy goes through his routine, talking about being single, working in a call centre and not having a real girlfriend for a very long time. Then finally, the last act comes onstage: Simon Worth, from the telly. There is loud clapping. He launches into a gag about gigs he's done on the road, then one about a corporate gig he had last week, and one about his hatred of wearing make-up for his 'telly' work. 'If wanted a makeover, I would've done a reality show, but I didn't. I signed up because I'm the best bloke for the job.'

Mary's notebook fills with comments describing Simon as he continues his set: extreme misogynist, horrible homophobe, racist bigot. The list reads like a list of illnesses or extinct animals.

She glances at the bar, thinking of all the things she would say to Corry if she were with her: 'Not funny, any of them. Couldn't they have learnt their lines instead of reading off the back of their hands? Have any of those boys got jobs? Do they even know what comedy is?'

When the gig's over, Mary stands outside the venue in the midnight dark. The feeling spreads through her, as it always does: the feeling of being violated.

When she gets home, the cat curls around her ankles and meows for food.

'Oh Roxy,' she says as she rubs beneath the cat's chin. 'You're funnier than all of those boys.'

She folds her pale slim hands around a strong cup of tea and spreads her feet into the comfort of her slippers. She eats hungrily: slices of cheese, apple and crackers. And thinks about that night when Corry said, 'I'm going to give it a go, Mum—comedy. I've always wanted to do it. There's a bar next to uni, they have an open-mic night. You never know, I might be the next Tina Fey.'

At the time, Mary didn't know much about comedy. She'd seen some things on telly, sit-coms, mainly American. Never laughed much, just watched them because there was nothing else on.

She scans the photographs on the mantelpiece—as she

always does when she comes in from a comedy night—taking in each image like the pages of a book: her life with Corry. Beaches, camping trips, toothless grins smiling out at her, the leggy early teens, all the hair styles and the mad clothes that Corry had loved. Just her and Corry, Corry's dad long gone.

Mary had tried to instil in Corry her love of walking in the Grampians, but it had never worked and often ended in tears or truncated trips. There's one shot of them together at the foot of Mount William, taken moments before eleven-year-old Corry had flatly refused to budge. They'd had their picnic in a park, instead of at the summit.

She looks at the last photo taken of Corry, grainy, out of focus, taken in a dark dingy comedy room. She's wearing a short black skirt, a denim jacket and lace up Doc Martin boots 'You look lovely, darling,' Mary had said to Corry.

'I've spent hours on this material—it's hilarious. See you in the morning, Mum.'

* * *

In the beginning, Corry was full of energy and pursued the idea of doing comedy like she did everything else, with a sense of fun and determination. Mary remembers her first gig: Corry was nervous and when she got back, she'd said, 'It wasn't great, but it wasn't bad'. Sometimes, before she went out, Mary would hear her rehearsing. She would smile with quiet pride at her guts for giving comedy a go.

After a while, though, when Corry returned from watching or doing comedy, she seemed agitated and annoyed.

'Why do you go?' Mary finally asked.

'Because I want to get better at doing comedy and these are the places you go to learn the craft.'

Mary had seen all of the school productions that Corry had been in but had never seen any of her comedy gigs. That was what Corry did with her friends. Besides, Corry had never asked Mary to come with her.

Afterwards, Mary found Corry's scribbled notes, in piles of spiral-bound notebooks. She hadn't kept Corry's clothes or shoes—the smell of them made her shake, nauseous with the enormous loss. But she cherished the words on the pages of those notebooks.

The first room Mary went to was in the northern suburbs, a big old pub, where high-profile comedians performed. There was a cover charge of $12 and if you paid more you could get a meal and a seat. Mary caught sight of herself in the mirror above the bar, her dark brown eyes looking perpetually like they were brimming with tears, the lines around her mouth and forehead forever crumpled in grief.

Mary didn't laugh once that night. Each act had got on stage, the men shouting and ranting racist remarks, and observations of politicians that were simplistic and crude. There was one woman who talked about her family in ways that Mary had found sad.

Mary was there because Corry had mentioned this room one night, her tone scathing: 'The guy who runs it,' she said in a sing-song voice, 'he said I'm not ready for a gig in his room. He patted my arm like he was tapping out Morse-code, 'not ready', dot, dot, dash, dash, dash, dash.'

Mary cried after she went to that first gig, holding some of Corry's notebooks to her, like a mother with a new-born. She wondered why her daughter was 'not ready,' for a gig. She wanted to ask the man who ran it, but he was famous, seemed busy and she felt silly at the thought of asking him.

A few weeks later, Mary went to a small room at the back of a pub. Some of Corry's lines were going round and round in her head. Sitting there in that badly lit room was awful. So many people around her, laughing at boorish boys who appeared to have regressed to a primitive state, failing understand what impact their words could have on others. Like foot soldiers in an unnamed war, they got up, one after the other and said more or less the same things, crudely, often with anger mapped across their faces. Some shouting, some leering and—almost without exception—completely artless, displaying an arrogance that Mary found alarming and repulsive. Calling women 'cunts'. Blaming refugees for their lack of employment. Citing the Holocaust as a display of German ingenuity.

Mary didn't cry into the box of notebooks when she got home that night. Instead she read all of them, carefully. The names of rooms, the names of the people who ran them, their numbers, often with comments next to them: 'no way', 'go back next week', 'need more experience'. There were numbers under two letters written on lots of pages: 'm' and 'w', she understood: 'm' meant 'men' and 'w' meant 'women' and the numbers beneath indicated how many of each performing at each gig. So few women and so very many men.

On the inside cover of one of the last notebooks, Corry had written 'not funny enough' again and again. The words were underlined, the pressure of the pen almost tearing through the page.

Mary remembered when Corry had come home one night, earlier than usual, with an odd look on her face. 'Agh! Those blokes are infuriating,' she had said. 'I get to the venue and tell them I'm there for the gig—it's taken me months to get a five-minute spot in that room, months—I get there, and they say, 'Oh sorry, love, but Gerry Marx has agreed to headline and the only way we can fit him in is to bump some people off the line-up.' Gerry freaking Marx, he isn't even funny, he just shouts and thrusts his crotch out. It's because he's on the bloody radio.'

Mary hadn't known what to say. It seemed unfair, but surely there were other rooms and other opportunities.

Corry had gone on. 'So I watch the first bracket, it's the usual suspects, Darren, Tim and that Kevin guy. They get spots everywhere, just turn up and get a spot, slap their mates on the back and get a gig. No other women, not one, and they bump me off. I've had it.'

Mary thinks back to that moment often: Corry was incensed, because she knew that she was just as funny as them, that she never read off the back of her hand and yet she could still only get a gig every now and again and that was after pestering the people who ran the rooms—they eventually gave her a gig just to shut her up.

And week after week, in other rooms, the truth of what had happened became clearer with each obscenity, with each casual sexist, racist, homophobic remark. All of them a provocation to Mary.

'I just want more stage time.' Corry had said. 'That's all. Like the blokes get. It's not a lot to ask for. Just two or three regular gigs in rooms, just to get better. I want to work up to do a show at the comedy festival. Imagine,' she'd grinned, 'me at the Melbourne International Comedy Festival. What a buzz.'

As the months went by, there were more stories: 'That dickhead who runs that room in Doncaster, when I got off the stage tonight, he said to the audience 'I don't know what the fuck that was, but she's got great tits.' Another time: 'That guy who runs that room in the city, he said I just wasn't funny and I never would be and maybe I should just go home and have babies instead.'

Mary would go into Corry's room and find her slumped over her laptop watching YouTube clips of comedians. It was a strange thing to see, like watching someone with an addiction. Corry was unhappy when she did comedy because of the way she was treated, and unhappy when she wasn't doing it because she loved it so much.

Mary began to amass a pile of her own notebooks with columns, headings and the plan sketched. She sat unnoticed, at the back of each room, and documented this world. It was purposeful. It didn't matter how late she stayed out: she was retired and there was only a shift at the op shopand if she couldn't do that, there was always someone else who could.

Like Corry, Mary went to rooms all over the city. At first, she thought maybe the first two were just an anomaly. But soon she realised that it was an entrenched pattern of behaviour. Occasionally a woman would appear like an apparition, a fleeting breath of fresh air, telling jokes about the men they had dated with incredible twists on themes of rape culture and feminism. Many of them nervously feeling their way through their lines.

The day the festival brochure is released, Mary scrutinises it. She reads the blurb for each of the 521 acts and cross-references each one with the venue where the act would be performed.

The acts are listed in alphabetical order and when Mary gets to the Cs, slow heavy tears roll down her cheeks, before the throbbing, jerking sobs begin. Corry's name should be there, her show, her image, right there, nestled among them all. Her shining, bright, funny Corry. When the sobs subside, Mary's resolve to enact her plan set like stone.

On the third night of the festival, Mary stands outside Melbourne Town Hall. When the last light goes down, she approaches the massive chalk board that advertises all the festival shows and starts her work. As the festival flags buffet in the wind above her, she rubs out 'Loaded' next to the first name, Simon Worth, and paints the word 'Misogynist' there instead. Removes the words 'Australia's Damned' from Kevin's show and replaces it with the word 'Bigot'. On and on, while her hand aches and her neck throbs, she rubs out and paints over a hundred show titles with:

'Homophobe.'

'Racist.'

'Sexist.'

'Anti-Semite.'

Her car is already packed. Backpack, camping gear, hiking clothes. She heads off early, feeling something other than despair for the first time in so very long. At the summit of Mount William, she looks out over the dense green and the craggy ancient landforms, then smiles as a pair of Gang Gang Cockatoos swoops past her. Their crests are a scarlet splash against the sandstone and their birdsong, an elongated creak, creak, like a cork being unwound from a good bottle of red wine.

Eurydice: Wide Justice

Men are afraid that women will laugh at them.
Women are afraid that men will kill them.

Margaret Atwood[70]

We exit the comedy room and stand looking up the deserted laneway. It is after 11pm.

'On 13 June 2018, 23-year-old Eurydice Dixon, a young comedian, walked home from a gig in a bar in Melbourne,' I tell The Group, who nods in recognition and acknowledgment. 'Eurydice was a rare comedian who made you sit up and listen: her jokes were well constructed, profound, political and deeply provocative. Eurydice was followed by a man as she walked home after her gig in the city. Eurydice was just moments away from her home when the man, who had followed her home, raped and murdered her. Eurydice wasn't murdered because she was a comedian, but her murder opened the door not just to discussions on what the comedy room environment is like but also how the environment can inhibit a sense of safety, how gigs are booked, the time slots that people are given and how comedians will get home afterwards. It also, of course, brought about yet more dialogue and debate about the broader and very complex issue of women's safety.'

The Group is motionless, each person clearly affected by the poignancy of the words in relation to the events in the comedy room we've just left, the dark alleyway, and the memory of Eurydice.

'The word Eurydice comes from the Greek for *Wide Justice*. In the aftermath of the murder, vigils across the country were held. From the open mic comedy scene in Melbourne, to the Melbourne International Comedy Festival, from the Victorian State parliament to the Edinburgh Festival, the brutal murder of the young and brilliant comedian Eurydice Dixon brought about many conversations and change. Eurydice's comedy was fearlessly feminist and funny in a way that made you really think.

'Many gigs across Melbourne were cancelled the night the news broke that Eurydice had been murdered. And many of us gathered in the bars where we performed comedy to share in the grief and the disbelief that someone in our community had been murdered. Because so many of us walk home after gigs, the implications for us all were very real, and the enormous sense of loss was heartbreaking.

'The room where I gathered with other comedians was a comedy room run by women. It felt good to be able to go somewhere and share the shock and the grief. We shared stories of gigs that we'd seen Eurydice do, and many talked

C.O.M.E.D.Y. Fact

Over 10,000 people gathered at a silent vigil in Princes Park and many thousands more gathered around Australia to say prayers and pay respect to Eurydice Dixon.

about times they had walked home late after a gig. For the first time in over a decade of doing stand-up comedy, I felt a strong sense of connection and community to many comedians who I had gigged with over the years. And together, days later we—with thousands of others—held each other at the silent vigil in Princes Park.[71]

'The overwhelming sense of disbelief and sadness was matched with a need to do something—not just in Melbourne, but across the international comedy scene. There were a number of initiatives across the world in response.

'*Chortle,* the most successful U.K. comedy forum for reviews and comedy industry commentary, conducted a survey asking comedians about their experience of safety in comedy rooms and when leaving comedy rooms. It was the first of its kind. More than 300 stand-ups took part in the *Chortle* survey, which asked questions about safety issues that comedians had experienced on and off the stage. The findings indicated that women experienced significant problems performing comedy in rooms and getting home after gigs. Over half of the women surveyed said they turned down work because they felt uncomfortable about another performer on the bill. Many suggested that a nominal fee could be offered to assist with transport costs after public transport stopped at night. Respondents wanted more women on the bill to stop the prevalence and ownership of comedy by straight white men. Female comedians wanted an environment where racist, sexist and offensive material was not tolerated. They wanted an environment where there were repercussions for offensive behaviour. Female comedians feel unsafe in environments where anything goes without repercussion.[72] The survey indicated that calling out bad behaviour and ensuring that there were repercussions would mean that the culture of comedy rooms could change, making them more welcoming and safer spaces for all.

'At the 2018 Edinburgh Fringe, an initiative called *The Home Safe Collective* was set up by Sameena Zehra, Angela Barnes and Pauline Eyre, in response to the murder of Eurydice. The collective used crowdfunding to pay for cab rides home so that women and non binary comedians could get home safely after a gig. In New Zealand, a similar initiative was implemented called *Get Me Home*, in response to a survey of female comedians that indicated that 51% of respondents turned down gigs because they felt unsafe getting home afterwards.

'At the 2019 Melbourne International Comedy Festival, two women on the open mic circuit, who knew Eurydice, gigged with her and also run an all-women's comedy night, implemented an initiative called *Light The Way Home*. Developed in partnership with Melbourne International Comedy Festival, *Light The Way Home* was in response to the fact that many performers who work late at night often don't earn enough money to cover the cost of transport. All these initiative were a huge shift and acknowledgement that doing live stand-up comedy in comedy rooms can be a hostile and prohibitive endeavour for women and minority groups.

'The increase in the number of women in comedy has resulted in informal avenues of support that women offer each other. Since Eurydice's murder, many of us make a conscious effort of going over to talk to other female comedians. There are rooms run by women; there are rooms that make a point of booking a diverse line-up. And amongst the women in the Melbourne comedy scene, we agreed to offer each other lifts, walk each other to tram stops, chip in for Ubers and cabs. We recognised that the hostility within comedy rooms is indicative of the wider gender-based violence.'

'Oy Vey, this is the most exhausting tour I've ever been on. But it's so good to know that the horror that Eurydice must have faced in her last hours of being alive has brought about change. And I hope that this brings some relief to Eurydice's family,' comments Ruth.

'Yes,' I reply. 'And in Eurydice's memory, her family and comedy friends set up The Awkward Giraffe, a non-profit that aims to promote critical comedy which engages with political social or philosophical issues. An incredible legacy,'[73] I tell the The Group.

'We're nearing the end of the tour,' I say. 'When we look back on it all, we can see how much has changed since the days of Diller and Rivers. There is the discourse, post-C.K. revelations, that called out the boys club comedy room environment. And the changes that came about after the murder of Eurydice Dixon. All of it highlighting the very real hostility faced by women and minorities in the comedy room environment and the inherent dangers of getting home after late night gigs. But look, before we disband, I want to ask you all: why do you think comedy and laughter matter?'

'It's about breaking taboos and holding those in power to account,' Ruth says.

'Isn't it?' Lucy replies. 'It's not just about getting laughs, comedy is like activism, it can help change what people think and do, it's joyful resistance'

'Tragedy plus time equals comedy: isn't that the saying? Imagine transforming all the bad things that have happened in your life into comedy, how cool would that be?' Andrew adds.

'Yes!' Ruth nods her head vigorously. 'Comedy does the heavy lifting. Imagine how powerful it must feel to walk into a room of strangers and make them laugh together as one.'

'It must be so addictive, you'd feel like a goddess with special powers.' Lucy stares dreamily into the middle distance.

Ruth smiles and holds her Egyptian cotton sheets close to her as a cool breeze floats down the laneway.

'Performance styles have changed, and the combative language traditionally used to describe comedy, like *die*, *kill* and *bomb* have been replaced by words like *connection* and *truth*. 'I'm not fighting you, I'm bringing you with me,'[74]

I say. 'And the comic 'is engaged in a painstakingly slow dialectical struggle with society's image of itself, never effecting change on a grand scale, yet, over time, gradually modulating the systems of power, much as a mutant gene precipitates a centuries-long process of evolution.'[75]

'It's important to note that for all of the shitty comedy rooms out there, there are also some well-run ones. They do exist! Seek them out.[76] And the creation of laughter? Well, it's a complex process within structures that have sought to exclude women from being funny. Making people laugh is a powerful thing to do, as it undermines those structures of oppression. When a woman steps up to the mic in a comedy room, there is the weight of history upon her, but her presence reshapes that history, gives her voice and the opportunity to use the vehicle of comedy to do all of that heavy historical lifting. And,' I add, 'Corrine Grant sums it up beautifully, when she says: "Freeing myself of the gender-specific prefix, here's what it's like to be a comedian: it is a job, it is a skill, it is a lot of smoke and mirrors. Stand-up comedy is an apprenticeship: you can't learn it from a book, you need to get up on stage and learn by doing it often, learn by failing at it. It's not for those of the faint-heart, the fragile ego, or false sense of identity. It is not for the slow-witted, but it is for those who are willing to pretend they are slow-witted. You must be brave, you must be committed, you must be willing to push boundaries, raise more questions than give answers and occasionally offend."[77]'

The Group agree to get a cab together, as it turns out that they all live close to one another. Ruth and Lucy exchange numbers.

'I want to be there when you do your first gig,' Ruth says.

'Ah yes, the first gig,' Lucy comments wistfully.

'I've learnt a lot,' Andrew says. 'The book will be a warts-and-all exposé on how tough it is to do comedy.' He flicks through his notes and shakes his head as if in disbelief.

I pause as The Group looks at me expectantly. 'That's it,' I declare. 'We are done! Thank you for coming along on the C.O.M.E.D.Y. Tour. It's been an absolute pleasure spending the time with you all.'

I watch them walk down the laneway, their arms filled with Egyptian cotton sheets and Droll Dolls. I roll up the HA! HA! Flag, place it in the basket on the back of my bike, and put my helmet on. Pedalling along the dark laneway, I make a mental note to add into the next tour that the increased number of women in comedy also reframes comedy itself. It's not enough to say that there has been a proliferation of women without clarifying the continuing issues for women based on racial and gendered lines and there is still a long way to go for there to be a fair representation of all women in comedy not just white women.

As I weave my way through the graffitied laneways, I consider that, because comedy has been a male domain for so long, women have been written off as not being funny.[78] But just because men find it difficult to reframe themselves out of being in the centre of every narrative, it doesn't mean that women can't create spaces for themselves, away from the deeply problematic environment that is a traditional comedy room.[79]

The cool night air cuts through the knowledge that although there has been a proliferation of women in comedy in recent times, this has not eradicated the inherent sexism in the industry, and certainly not mitigated violence against women. But the increase of the number of women in comedy is marked, and women on line-ups in comedy rooms are becoming the norm rather than the exception.

I cycle up the steady incline of Bourke Street, riding past a long-standing comedy room which often gets called out on Twitter for the imbalance in the number of men and women they book on their open mic nights. These callouts are like a public shaming and although they don't always translate to changes in rooms, it sends a strong message that the behaviour is no longer acceptable. I see a poster for the forthcoming gig in the room and ponder on the discriminatory gatekeeping in

C.O.M.E.D.Y. Facts

The maker of the pod cast** The Guilty Feminist**, by Deborah Frances—White, was initially pitched to the BBC, but it wasn't funded—because the BBC said no one would listen to it—so Deborah produced it independently.** The Guilty Feminist **has been downloaded over sixty million times.

comedy rooms considering what is actually at stake: a five-minute set in a bar with no pay.

As I round the corner onto Spring Street, the flags heralding the opening of another blockbuster show flutter across the façade of the magnificent Princess Theatre. I consider the increased number of platforms afforded to everyone, regardless of their gender, away from the tightly held spaces that are small comedy rooms down dark alley ways, in bars, upstairs in pubs and tucked away at the back of pool rooms across Melbourne. Relatively new platforms like Instagram TV, Tik Toc, YouTube channels, and podcasts have led to a democratisation of comedy opportunities allowing anyone to 'make it' on their own terms.

Pedalling over to the Carlton Gardens, I reflect on the huge success of shows like *The Katering Show,* by comedians Kate McCartney and Kate McLennan, which was originally released on YouTube as a web series and clocked over a million views, then went on to mainstream success. And the other female-led comedic enterprises like the incredibly popular podcast *The Guilty Feminist,* which coined the phrase 'I'm a feminist but,'[80] which is stated at the start of each episode. All of them eroding the male topography of comedy.

I head up Rathdowne Street and merge onto the Park Street bike path, the oncoming lights of other cyclists piercing the darkness. The ride is easy now, and I'm nearly home as I reflect on the long-held belief that women aren't funny. That, I think, should simply be reframed into women aren't funny in relation to men. And the increasing number of access points to do stand-up comedy away from comedy rooms ensures that more women enter and remain in comedy.

At Sydney Road, I glance momentarily into the inky expanse of Princes Park. I know that oppression of women continues, but from that oppression women's humour arises.[81] And is a constant reminder of how powerful comedy can be.

It's quiet now, just the odd car whooshing past. Instinctively, I look behind me as I dismount from my bike and walk over to where I chain it up for the night. Maybe there will never be industrial laws that govern comedy rooms, but despite this more women are doing comedy than ever before. And the holy grail of learning the ropes of how to do stand-up comedy is no longer exclusively bound to the gruelling process of standing up with a mic on a rickety stage in front of a group of strangers, or—worse still—a group of young guys who are giving comedy a go.

I touch my fingers to my lips and press them lightly to the mezuzah of the door to my apartment and give thanks to the comedians, philosophers, thinkers and activists who have come before me or walked with me, who have reconstructed the joke envelope, revealed oppression, exclusion and danger under the sharp glare of the footlights in a comedy room. The voices that have challenged the 'norms' of the world of comedy.

These people have presented me with ideas, truths,

explanations and stories that have helped me understand that out of oppression comes a strong chorus of voices. Some are earnest, some are erudite, some offer up polemics and some soar with the power to make people laugh.

Sadly some voices will always remain unheard. I let myself into my apartment, go over to my desk and continue working on a short story set in a growth corridor in the Northern suburbs of Melbourne.

Stage Five

'Lucy, it's so lovely to see you again. The weeks just fly by, don't they?' Jennifer shakes her head and tuts.

The door shuts behind them with a quiet click. A series of black-and-white framed photographs of Lucy's children, Logan and Grace, cover the length of the hallway. Jennifer's heels echo off the timber boards as they make their way into the expansive open-plan living-dining-kitchen area. The stove top and fridge match the steel gleam of the sink, and the arc suspended over the sink is like a precision instrument rather than a tap. Above the faux fireplace is another black-and-white framed image—a wedding shot of Lucy and Gregg adopting a Gone With The Wind style embrace. Light floods in via floor to ceiling glass sliding doors. Beyond the glass doors, there is a covered outdoor dining area and a patch of astro-turf replete with parked tricycles and a timber cubby house.

Lucy flicks on the kettle and raises her arm to open one of the overhead cupboards filled with an array of teas. Lucy's low-rise jeans are moulded over a gym-toned body, and the soft folds of her cotton striped shirt sit tastefully across her slender frame.

'Oh, no tea, thank you,' Jennifer says.

Lucy lowers her arm slowly.

'I just had a coffee before I left the office.' Jennifer removes her Clovac-branded jacket and places it next to her as she perches on the edge of a deep leather couch. She pulls out an iPad from her bag.

'Well, the questions are the same as last week really, with the exception of question eight. We need more of a reflective answer to that one.' She nods as Lucy sits next to her. Lucy and Jennifer could be mistaken for sisters: straightened hair, slim builds and eyebrows plucked into precise arches.

'As usual, I just have to read you the Clovac survey disclaimer first. 'As the appointed Woodlakes Residents' Representative, your responses to the social planning tool survey will be utilized as a metric against the asset-based community development framework which will inform the next stages of Woodlakes. Your responses are anonymous, and your input is appreciated.'' Jennifer smiles briefly.

'Question one: On a scale of one to twenty-seven, would you say that the house design you have chosen at Woodlakes gives you a feeling of belonging and exclusivity at the same time? Twenty-seven being something you could swear a pledge to and one being something you would consider taking action against to ensure that change occurred.'

Lucy is the appointed Residents' Reference Group

spokesperson principally because she and Gregg were the first to include a wok burner and a double sink in their outdoor setting in the stage one development. Lucy knows that her responses could mean the difference between pendant lighting or downlights in subsequent stages of the Woodlakes development.

'Oh, twenty-five, definitely twenty-five,' Lucy replies, her left knee bobbing up and down as if an infant were upon it, the shoe on her slim foot slipping off at the heel revealing a tiny gecko tattoo curling round her heel.

'Question two: Over the last week, how many other Woodlakes residents have you interacted with? Naught to five, five or more, or in excess of five?' Jennifer asks.

'I saw the people from number 9 leave the other morning, when I looked out from Logan's window as I was changing his nappy. There were five of them getting into the car. But I haven't actually spoken to anyone.'

The hum of the baby monitor on the kitchen bench is disturbed by a murmur. Jennifer glances towards the noise.

Lucy blushes slightly, 'Sorry. Sometimes they wake then settle themselves back to sleep.'

'Adorable. I'm sure that they are just adorable.' Jennifer taps her painted nail against the screen. 'This won't take long, questions three to seven require a yes or no answer and the final question is your opportunity to give that reflective response, which, as you know may be used in future promotional material.'

Now the children are bawling and sputtering with intermittent gasps. Jennifer pointedly exhales, jabbing her finger against the screen as she inputs Lucy's responses.

'I'll be quick with this last question. There's a play area earmarked for stage five of the Woodlakes Development. Would you as a resident with younger children consider that the inclusion of an exercise park within the play area would be something that would prohibit family interaction, or encourage neighbourly connection? We want you to give a reflective answer. But really,' she glances in the direction of the baby monitor, 'feel free just to say yes or no.'

'Sorry.' Lucy hesitates, then turns the volume down on the baby monitor. 'An exercise park? Oh, I think that would be a really great drawcard. The gym is a good forty-minutes' drive away, so an exercise park would definitely encourage neighbourly connection.'

'Lovely,' Jennifer snaps shut her tablet, puts it in her bag and insists that there is no need for Lucy to come to the door with her.

Grace and Logan smear yogurt across the tables of their highchairs and gawp at the movie Frozen which is on the immense screen in front of them.

Lucy nibbles on left over crusts from their vegemite sandwiches while she packs nappies, wipes, and snacks into the large bag that hangs off the stroller. She went into a panic because she discovered that there was only a smear left at the bottom of the jar of nappy cream, when she went to change their nappies after Jennifer had left. Grace and Logan's faces were a red blur of anguish at having been left to cry for so long. And Logan had pink welts of a bad case of nappy rash all over his bum, with not enough nappy cream in the house to sooth it.

Lucy clips each child into their seat and adjusts screens in front of their respective monitor stands. She pushes the double stroller out onto the slate pathway. In the centre of her garden, water cascades over blue ceramic orbs onto granite stones. Each house has its own unique garden feature: particular shaped steppingstones, selected verdant miniature bushes and a distinctive water feature.

Lucy hasn't walked anywhere since they moved into Woodlakes fourteen months ago. Her normal routine is to drive to the gym twice a week at eight pm and to the supermarket every Monday, once Gregg gets in from work. All of the activities with the children, like driving to parks and visiting friends, is done at the weekend as a family.

Eucalypt Boulevard curves into Grevilia Lane. A brown-haired man grins maniacally holding up two thumbs and raving about the NBN roll-out, on a poster that is being inserted into a display screen of a bus shelter. As Lucy approaches, the clips around the screen are snapped shut and two men in orange overalls drive off in their work van. The Woodlakes residents have been assured that as soon as stage five of Woodlakes is completed, the bus service will commence. Until then, the posters are the only things that come and go.

Lucy pulls back the hood of the stroller and checks that the children still have their sun hats on. Each of them stares fixedly at their screens. As she leans further over the stroller to adjust Logan's hat, her lower rib cage nudges the handle of the stroller. She inhales quickly, bites her bottom lip, straightens up and exhales slowly.

Lucy has only seen stage five of Grevillia Lane on the promotional brochures that Jennifer occasionally brings with her. The brochures assure new residents that at every stage of development, peace and tranquillity is assured, even as the building works progress.

Lucy knows from experience though, that no matter what stage families are at, once they are inside their homes, a passing car is whisper-quiet, rubbish bins being trundled out for collection are barely audible, and a woman's scream cannot be heard.

Punchline

I know, that's a pretty grim story to end on, my point is that gender-based violence is at epidemic proportions. There are so many subtle, entrenched and pervasive systems and structures that silence and undermine women, from darkly lit comedy rooms to federal politics, to horrific acts of violence globally which prohibit girls from being educated.

Initially I had a complex and conflicted relationship with comedy, from that first gig—the gateway drug. In the early years I was harnessing my well-worn relationship with fear, failure and humiliation. Comedy is a great vehicle for that. I expected to fail at everything, not just comedy. Performing allowed me to encounter humiliation and have to harness my fear of the said inevitability of failure and humiliation. It never felt gutsy or brave doing comedy, just a compulsion to encounter those emotions again and again and to sit in the exquisite torture of comedy perdition.

For many years I never thought I was 'funny enough,' smart enough, quick enough and I was certainly not on the scene enough. The scene being the badly lit comedy rooms. I started doing comedy when my youngest child was eighteen months old. I went out once a week to watch and or perform comedy. I simply was not able to put in the work to get better fast. And each and every time I was in a room I felt this odd sense of being excluded, of being undermined, sometimes subtly sometimes overtly by the other comedians, mainly male. I couldn't see me there. If you can see it you can be it right? I just couldn't see me. I saw a parade of twenty something males performing on the whole un-crafted material, and yet progressing through the 'ranks,' going from five-minute spots, to MC to headline. For many years, I felt like I was standing very still.

Over time I began to harness the drivers that lead me to comedy, the fear the failure the sense of humiliation, so that I controlled them. I became shameless about getting gigs at conferences, at events. I wrote show after show. Performed at comedy festivals. I was in a marriage where I didn't feel seen. Comedy allowed me to be heard, to be seen. I loved the challenge of writing festival shows, setting up the premise and working out the narrative arch.

Creating shows that reflected where I was at, at the time; *Pain Sans Frontier* (bread without borders) (MICF 2012) a show that pondered what if Mrs Piaget had written Piaget's cognitive theory of early childhood, asking if she had written the theory, would she have used words like concrete and operational? And could Mrs Piaget have answered the ultimate posser 'why don't children eat their crusts?'

In Bench Press, a kitchen – sink drama. Bench Press was the new feminist publishing house. I took the audience for a rolling pin ride through first wave, second wave feminism through to twenty-first century Microwave feminism, which is for the time poor but theory rich, seminal, polemic and always on defrost.

And on and on. Through to creating the Melbourne Jewish Comedy Festival. And yet it wasn't until I began to research comedy did I understand how difficult it was for a woman to do comedy. To be seen and heard, to create that moment, that glorious moment of alchemy, of making people laugh.

My relationship with comedy is complex, profound and life changing. As a Jew humour is in my DNA and once I accepted that I would not have a stellar rise to commercial success and just had to lean into it, finding and creating opportunities to perform and look at it from every angle, then I began finally after nearly two decades to enjoy the art form.

Comedy has taken me emotionally spiritually, intellectually and geographically to places I could never have imagined. It helps me distil what I see and feel around me. It got me through a tough few years in a long marriage, which I left towards the end of finishing my research on gender and comedy. The research helped me understand why that initial foray into comedy was so fraught and why those spaces were and still are complex and exclusive.

I think that we are only as good as our last joke. But we are also the sum of the whole.

I think every woman should do comedy. It's a tough gig, but it is a powerful artform that gives us agency over our stories and can undermine the systems and structures that seek to undermine us. And slowly over time effects a change.

I leave you with this from Joan Rivers:

'Part of my act is meant to shake you up. It looks like I'm being funny, but I'm reminding you of other things. Life is tough, darling. Life is hard. And we better laugh at everything; otherwise, we're going down the tube.'[82]

Notes

1 Oliver Double, 'Tragedy Plus Time: Transforming Life Experience into Stand-Up Comedy', 143–55

2 Arthur Asa Berger, 'Three Holy Men Get Haircuts: The Semiotic Analysis of a Joke', 489

3 Sigmund Freud, *Jokes And Their Relation to The Unconscious*, 100

4 Henri Bergson, *Laughter, An Essay On The Meaning of the Comic*, 65

5 Natalie Meisner and Donia Mounsef, 'Gender, Humour and Transgression in Canadian Women's Theatre', 49

6 Meisner & Mounsef, 51

7 Mary J Russo, *The Female Grotesque: Risk, Excess and Modernity*, 54

8 'Carnivalesque', *Oxford Reference* [online].

9 Mikhail Bakhtin, *Rabelais and His World*, 65

10 Linda Mizjejewski, *Pretty/Funny: Women and Body Politics*, 22

11 Sigmund Freud, *Jokes And Their Relation to The Unconscious*, 97

12 Eliza Skinner, 'Famous Dick Jokes Are Just the Tip of the Problem'

13 Bridget Boyle, 'Take Me Seriously. Now Laugh at Me! How Gender Influences the Creation of Contemporary Physical Comedy', 79

14 Alenka Zupančič, *The Odd One In: On Comedy*, 137

15 Judith Butler, 'Performative Acts and Gender Constitution: An Essay in Phenomenology and Feminist Theory', 520

16 *Ibid.*, 520

17 *Ibid.*

18 *Ibid.*, 526

19 *Ibid.*, 184

20 Sigmund Freud, *Jokes And Their Relation to The Unconscious*, 104

21 Joanne R. Gilbert, 'Performing Marginality: Comedy, Identity, and Cultural Critique', 318

22 *Ibid.*, 319

23 Alexandra Petri, '10 Classic Phyllis Diller One-liners'.

24 Patrick Hatch, 'The 26 Best Joan Rivers Quotes'

25 Sharon Lockyer, 'From Toothpick Legs to Dropping Vaginas: Gender and Sexuality in Joan Rivers' Stand-up Comedy

Performance', 117

26 Susan Horowitz, *Queens of Comedy: Lucille Ball, Phyllis Diller, Carol Burnett, Joan Rivers, and the New Generation of Funny Women*, 103

27 Ellie Tomsett, 'Positives and Negatives: Reclaiming the Female Body and Self-deprecation in Stand-up Comedy', 10

28 Regina Barreca, *Laughs Perspectives on Women and Comedy*, 19

29 Mary J Russo, *The Female Grotesque: Risk, Excess and Modernity*, 54

30 Veronica Lee, 'Alternative comedy's greatest makes a very welcome return to stand-up as an MC'

31 Bridget Christie, *A Book For Her and Him If He Can Read*, 71

32 *Ibid.*, 71

33 Joanne R. Gilbert, 'Performing Marginality: Comedy, Identity, and Cultural Critique', 326

34 Debra Aarons and Marc Mierowsky, 'Obscenity, Dirtiness and Licence in Jewish Comedy', 174

35 Shaina Hammerman, 'Dirty Jews: Amy Schumer and Other Vulgar Jewesses', 52

36 Sarah Silverman, *Jesus Is Magic*

37 Shaina Hammerman, 'Dirty Jews: Amy Schumer and Other Vulgar Jewsses', 51.

38 ay', *Wealthy Gorilla*, <https://wealthygorilla.com/amy-schumer-quotes/>, accessed 20 May 2020

39 *Marvellous Mrs. Maisel*, Season 2, Episode 2, Amazon Prime, 2017

40 Adrienne Truscott, 'Asking For It'

41 Steph Harmon, 'Nakkiah Lui on gender, race and her new comedy show: "What if your vagina came to life?"'

42 Melena Rizak, 'The Comedy-Destroying, Soul-Affirming Art of Hannah Gadsby'

43 Email from Pietta Farrell, Melbourne International Comedy Festival, 5 April 2019

44 Eliza Skinner, 'Famous Dick Jokes are Just the Tip of the Problem'

45 Melanie Piper, 'Louis C.K.'s Time's Up Time Out: Rereading Persona Post-Scandal'

46 Marc Maron, 'Kim Deal'

47 Laurie Kilmartin, 'Being a Female in Louis C.K.'s World'

48 Megh Wright, 'We Always Knew a Louis C.K. Comeback Would Be Easy'

49 Sigmund Freud, *Jokes and Their Relation to the Unconscious*, 117

50 Joanne Brookfield, *No Apologies*, 64.

51 Ruth Cherrington, *Not Just Beer and Bingo, A Social History of Working Men's Clubs*, xi

52 Kate Fox, Stand Up and Be (En)Countered Resistance in solo stand-up performance by Northern English women, 84

53 *Ibid.*,12

54 *Ibid.*, 80

55 Lindy West, *Shrill Notes From A Loud Woman*, 210

56 *Ibid.*, 191

57 *Ibid.*

58 David Grossman, *A Horse Walks into a Bar*

59 Lindy West, *Shrill Notes From A Loud Woman*

60 Joanne Brookfield, *No Apologies*

61 Oliver Double, 'Teaching Stand-up Comedy: a Mission Impossible?', 16

62 *Ibid.*, 16

63 Simone de Beauvoir, *The Second Sex*, 138

64 Joanne Brookfield, *No Apologies*, 51

65 Fran De Groen & Peter Kirkpatrick (eds), *Serious Frolic Essays on Australian Humour*, 202

66 Joanne Brookfield, *No Apologies*, 61

67 Joanne R Gilbert, 'Performing Marginality: Comedy, Identity, and Cultural Critique', 318

68 Lindy West, *Shrill Notes From A Loud Woman*, 190

69 Interviews with Melbourne-based stand-up comics were conducted for my MA research, with Ethics Approval Number [E17-045], La Trobe University. Names throughout are withheld for reasons of confidentiality. Extracts from transcripts, April 2018

70 Margaret Atwood, *Curious Pursuits: Occasional Writing*, 2

71 Mark Stewart, 'Boxes of tissues circulated at Princes Park where mourners gathered to farewell Eurydice Dixon' [image], *Daily Mercury* [online], 19 June 2018

72 'One in Four Female Comedians has been Molested', *Chortle*, 2 August 2018, <https://www.chortle.co.uk, accessed 24 September 2018

73 Jeremy Dixon, 'Thoughts on Ouspensky and Humour'

74 Joanne Brookfield, *No Apologies*, 230

75 Bridget Boyle, 'Take Me Seriously. Now Laugh at Me! How Gender Influences the Creation of Contemporary Physical Comedy', 51

76 Joanne Brookfield, *No Apologies*, 63

77 Corinne Grant, 'Professional Comedian: Gender Has Nothing To Do With it'

78 Joanne Brookfield, *No Apologies*, 117

79 *Ibid.*

80 *Guilty Feminist* [podcast]

81 Sevda Caliskan, 'Is There Such a Thing as Women's Humor?', 58

82 Kim Quindlen, '57 Quotes From The Best Female Comedians Of All Time'

Bibliography

Aarons, Debra and Mierowsky, Marc 'Obscenity, Dirtiness and Licence in Jewish Comedy', *Comedy Studies*, 5/2 (2014), 174

Asa Berger, Arthur, 'Three Holy Men Get Haircuts: The Semiotic Analysis of a Joke', *Europe's Journal of Psychology*, 12/ 3 (2016), 489

Atwood, Margaret, *Curious Pursuits: Occasional Writing* (London: Hachette, 2000), 2

Bergson, Henri, *Laughter: An Essay On The Meaning of the Comic* (New York: The Macmillan Company, 1912)

Bakhtin, Mikhail, *Rabelais and His World* (Cambridge, MA: MIT Press, 1968), 65

Barreca, Regina, *Laughs Perspectives on Women and Comedy* (New York: Gordon and Breach, 1988), 19

Boyle, Bridget, 'Bits and Bumps: Understanding Gender in Contemporary Physical Comedy', PhD thesis (Queensland University of Technology, 2015)

Boyle, Bridget, 'Take Me Seriously. Now Laugh at Me! How Gender Influences the Creation of Contemporary Physical Comedy', *Comedy Studies*, 6/2 (2015), 78–90

Brookfield, Joanne, *No Apologies* (London: Echo Publishing, 2019)

Butler, Judith, 'Performative Acts and Gender Constitution: An Essay in Phenomenology and Feminist Theory', *Theatre Journal*, 40/4 (1988), 519–31

Butler, Judith, *Gender Trouble: Feminism and the Subversion of Identity* (New York: Routledge, 1990)

Caliskan, Sevda, 'Is There Such a Thing as Women's Humor?', *American Studies International*, 33/2 (1995), 49–59

'Carnivalesque', *Oxford Reference* [online], https://www.oxfordreference.com/view/10.1093/oi/authority.20110803095550811, accessed 24 November 2019

Cherrington, Ruth, *Not Just Beer and Bingo: A Social History of Working Men's Clubs* (Bloomington, Indiana: AuthorHouse, 2012)

Christie, Bridget, *A Book For Her and Him If He Can Read* (London: Penguin, 2015)

Colangelo, Anthony, 'Brutal murder of Australian comedian Eurydice Dixon shocks community', *Stuff* [online],17 June 2018.

<https://www.stuff.co.nz/world/australia/104780108/flowers-tears-a-minutes-silence-for-young-australian-murder-victim-eurydice-dixon.html >, accessed 9 Feb. 2021

Condron, Stephanie, 'Women Win Equality at Working Men's Clubs', *Telegraph* [online], 2 April 2007, <https://www.telegraph.co.uk/news/uknews/1547345/Women-win-equality-at-working-mens-clubs.html>, accessed 10 June 2016

De Beauvoir, Simone, *The Second Sex* (London: Vintage, Random House, 1949)

De Groen, Fran and Kirkpatrick, Peter (eds), *Serious Frolic Essays on Australian Humour* (Queensland: University of Queensland Press, 2009)

Dixon, Jeremy, 'Thoughts on Ouspensky and Humour', *The Awkward Giraffe* [blog], (9 April 2020) <https://www.awkwardgiraffe.com.au/2019/04/09/ouspensky-and-humour/>, accessed 19 Apr. 2020

Double, Oliver, 'Teaching Stand-up Comedy: a Mission Impossible?', *Studies in Theatre and Performance*, 20/1 (2000), 14–23

Double, Oliver, 'Tragedy Plus Time: Transforming Life Experience into Stand-up Comedy', *New Theatre Quarterly*, 33/2 (2017), 143–55

Double, Oliver, 'The Origin of the Term 'Stand-up Comedy' – update', *Comedy Studies*, 9/2 (2018), 235–37

Farrell, Pietta, email; Melbourne International Comedy Festival, 5 April 2019

Fox, Kate, 'How Stand-ups Construct and are Constructed by the "Northernness Effect"', *Comedy Studies Journal,* 9/1 (2018), 19–35

Fox, Kate, 'Stand Up and Be (En)Countered Resistance in solo stand-up performance by Northern English women, marginalised on the basis of gender, class and regional identity', PHD Thesis (University of Leeds 2017)

Freud, Sigmund, *Jokes and Their Relation to the Unconscious* (London: Butler and Tanner, 1960)

Gilbert, Joanne R, 'Performing Marginality: Comedy, Identity, and Cultural Critique', *Text and Performance Quarterly*, 17/4 (1997), 317–30

Grant, Corinne, 'Professional Comedian: Gender Has Nothing to do With it', *ABC News* [online], 26 April 2011, <http://www.abc.net.au/news/2011-04-26/grant—gender-and-comedy/167332>, accessed 24 March 2017

Grossman, David, *A Horse Walks into a Bar* (Vintage, 2017)

Guilty Feminist [podcast], <https://guiltyfeminist.com>, accessed 15 December 2019

Hammerman, Shaina, 'Dirty Jews: Amy Schumer and Other Vulgar Jewesses' in Steven J Ross (ed.), Michael Renov & Vincent Brook (guest eds) and Lisa Ansell (associate ed.), *From Shtetl to Stardom: Jews and Hollywood—the Jewish Role in American Life: An Annual Review* (Indiana: Purdue Press, 2017), 49–71

Harmon, Steph, 'Nakkiah Lui on gender, race and her new comedy show: 'What if your vagina came to life?', *Guardian* [online], 4 December 2017, <https://www.theguardian.com/tv-and-radio/2017/dec/04/nakkiah-lui-on-gender-race-and-her-new-comedy-show-what-if-your-vagina-came-to-life>, accessed 6 December 2017

Hatch, Patrick, 'The 26 Best Joan Rivers Quotes', *Sydney Morning Herald* [online], 5 September 2014, <https://www.smh.com.au/entertainment/celebrity/the-26-best-joan-rivers-quotes-20140905-3ex9p.html>, accessed 17 November 2019

Hollander, Jenny, '13 Hannah Gadsby 'Nanette' Quotes You Won't Be Able To Stop Thinking About', *Marie Claire* [online], 20 July 2018, <https://www.marieclaire.com/culture/a22502991/hannah-gadsby-nanette-quotes/>, accessed 18 June 2019

Horowitz, Susan, *Queens of Comedy: Lucille Ball, Phyllis Diller, Carol Burnett, Joan Rivers, and the New Generation of Funny Women* (London and New York : Routledge, 1997)

Jewell, Hannah, 'Weird and Excellent Thoughts about Gender and Babies', *Buzzfeed*, 19 August 2016, <https://www.buzzfeed.com/hannahjewell/weird-and-excellent-thoughts-about-gender-and-babies>, accessed 23 March 2019

Kilmartin, Laurie, 'Being a Female in Louis C.K.'s World', *New York Times* [online], 10 November 2017. <https://www.nytimes.com/2017/11/10/opinion/sunday/louis-ck-harassment.html?mwrsm=Email>, accessed 10 November 2017

Lee, Veronica, 'Alternative comedy's greatest makes a very welcome return to stand-up as an MC', *The Arts Desk*, 29 January 2012, <https://theartsdesk.com/comedy/alexei-sayle-soho-theatre>, accessed 10 February 2020

Lee-Kennedy, Brydie, 'Men Look After Men: Sexism and Domestic Abuse in the Australian Comedy Community', *SBS Comedy* [online], 3 December 2015, <http://www.sbs.com.au/comedy/article/2015/12/03/men-look-after-men-sexism-and-domestic-abuse-

australian-comedy-community>, accessed 20 November 2016 (now inactive)

Lockyer, Sharon, 'From Toothpick Legs to Dropping Vaginas: Gender and Sexuality in Joan Rivers' Stand-up Comedy Performance', *Comedy Studies Journal*, 2/2 (2011), 113–23

Maron, Marc, 'Kim Deal', *WTF with Marc Maron* [podcast], 13 November 2017, <http://www.wtfpod.com/podcast/episode-863-kim-deal?rq=kim%20deal>, accessed 29 January 2019

Marvellous Mrs. Maisel, Amazon Prime, 2017 [television program]

Meisner, Natalie and Mounsef, Donia, 'Gender, Humour and Transgression in Canadian Women's Theatre', *Prague Journal of English Studies*, 3/1 (2014), 47–64

Mizejewski, Linda, *Pretty/Funny: Women Comedians and Body Politics* (Austin: University of Texas Press, 2014)

Moore, Lisa, 'The Marvellous Mrs Maisel might be set in the 1960s but the story is still true for female comedians today', *Conversation*, 14 December 2017, <https://theconversation.com/amp/the-marvelous-mrs-maisel-might-be-set-in-the-1960s-but-the-story-is-still-true-for-female-comedians-today-87282>, accessed 14 December 2017

'One in Four Female Comedians has been Molested', *Chortle*, 2 August 2018, <https://www.chortle.co.uk/news/2018/08/02/40648/one_in_four_female_comedians_has_been_molested>, accessed 24 September 2018

Petri, Alexandra, '10 Classic Phyllis Diller One-liners', *Washington Post* [online], 20 August 2012, <https://www.washingtonpost.com/blogs/compost/post/ten-classic-phyllis-diller-one-liners/2012/08/20/0876f86c-eb0c-11e1-a80b-9f898562d010_blog.html>, accessed 24 Nov. 2019

Piper, Melanie, 'Louis C.K.'s Time's Up Time Out: Rereading Persona Post-Scandal', *Celebrity Studies Journal*, 10, 264–66 (2019)

Quindlen, Kim, '57 Quotes From The Best Female Comedians Of All Time—On Confidence, Integrity, And Fighting For What You Believe In,' Thought Catalogue [online], 3 August 2015, https://thoughtcatalog.com/kim-quindlen/2015/08/57-quotes-from-the-best-female-comedians-of-all-time-confidence-life-integrity-hard-work/, accessed 24 November 2019

Riviere, Joan, 'Womanliness as a Masquerade', *The International Journal of Psycho-Analysis*, Vol. 10 (1929), 303

Rizak, Melena, 'The Comedy-Destroying, Soul-Affirming Art of Hannah Gadsby', *New York Times* [online], 24 July 2018, <https://www.nytimes.com/2018/07/24/arts/hannah-gadsby-comedy-nanette.html>, accessed 28 August 2018

Rowe, Kathleen, *The Unruly Woman: Gender and Genres of Laughter* (Texas: University of Texas Press, 2011)

Russell, Danielle, 'Self-deprecatory Humour and the Female Comic: Self-destruction or Comedic Construction?', *Third Space: A Journal of Feminist Theory and Culture,* 1/2 (2002), retrieved from <https://journals.sfu.ca/thirdspace/index.php/journal/article/view/d_russell/68, accessed> June 2018

Russo, Mary J., *The Female Grotesque: Risk, Excess and Modernity* (New York: Routledge, 1995)

Silverman, Sarah, *Jesus Is Magic* [film] (Roadside Attractions, 2005)

Skinner, Eliza, 'Famous Dick Jokes are Just the Tip of the Problem', *Refinery*, 15 November 2017, <https://www.refinery29.com/amp/2017/11/180992/eliza-skinner-sexual-harassment-female-comedians>, accessed 17 November 2017

Smith, Nicola, 'Murder of Australian Comedian Sparks Outcry'. *The Telegraph* [online], 18 June 2018. <https://www.telegraph.co.uk/news/2018/06/15/ murder-australian-comedian-sparks-outcry-violence-against-women/>, accessed 9 February 2021

Smith, Rohan, '"Disrespectful" Moment at Eurydice Vigil', *Daily Mercury* [online], 19 June 2018, <https://www.dailymercury.com.au/news/silence-broken-at-memorial-for-eurydice-dixon-by-j/3445916/>, accessed 28 November 2018

Stewart, Mark, 'Boxes of tissues circulated at Princes Park where mourners gathered to farewell Eurydice Dixon' [image], *Daily Mercury* [online], 19 June 2018, <https://www.dailymercury.com.au/news/silence-broken-at-memorial-for-eurydice-dixon-by-j/3445916/>, accessed 28 November 2018

Taylor, John Matthew, 'Outside Looking In: Stand-up Comedy, Rebellion, and Jewish Identity in Early Post-World War II America', MA thesis (Indiana University, 2010)

Tomsett , Ellie, 'Positives and Negatives: Reclaiming the Female Body and Self-deprecation in Stand-up Comedy. *Comedy Studies Journal,* 9/1 (2018), 6–18

Truscott, Adrienne, 'Asking For It', *Adrienne Truscott* [online] 2019, <http://www.adriennetruscott.com/asking-for-it>, accessed 29 August 2019

Wallin, Emmy, '32 Hilarious Amy Schumer Quotes to Brighten Your Day', *Wealthy Gorilla*, <https://wealthygorilla.com/amy-schumer-quotes/>, accessed 20 May 2020

West, Lindy, *Shrill: Notes From a Loud Woman.* (London: Hachette, 2016)

West, Lindy, 'Why Men Aren't Funny', *New York Times* [online], 14 November 2017, <https://www.nytimes.com/2017/11/14/opinion/louis-ck-not-funny-harassment.html>, accessed 14 November 2017

Wright, Megh, 'We Always Knew A Louis C.K. Comeback Would Be Easy', *Vulture*, 31 October 2018, <https://www.vulture.com/2018/10/we-always-knew-a-louis-c-k-comeback-would-be-easy.html>, accessed November 2018

Zoglin, Richard, *Comedy At The Edge: How Stand-up in the 1970s Changed America* (New York: Bloomsbury, 2009)

Zoglin, Richard, 'Stand-up Comedy', *Encyclopaedia Britannica* [online], 2017, <https://www.britannica.com/art/stand-up-comedy>, accessed 28 March 2018

Zupančič, Alenka, *The Odd One In: On Comedy* (Cambridge, MA; London: MIT Press, 2008)

Acknowledgments

None of this would have happened if it weren't for my friend and writing mentor Angela Savage who said, 'I know you can.'

Numerous friends, family members, writers and editors have listened, supported and held my hand throughout the process. To you all, thank you for your friendship and patience: Deb Rechter, Bronwyn Lay, Karen Feldman, Karen Glasson, Jennifer Andersen, Dee Wild, Noe Harsel, Maryanne Netto, Paul Teasdale, Helen Gaynor, Toni Sless, Georgia Cremin, Irene Myers, David Sless, Peter Peverley, Keith Thompson, Tony Birch, Emma Cayley, Julie Twohig, Janelle Dunstan, Tegan Connelly, Sabine Minatta, Kate Mullin, Rabbi Dovid Gutnick and Rachel Gutnick. To my incredible supervisors at La Trobe University Alison Ravenscroft and Juliane Roemhild—thank you.

To all of the comedians whom I have talked to and gigged with: together we have made a difference to so many places doing that thing we all love—comedy—in comedy rooms where our presence has made it so much easier for the next woman who walks into the bar. Legends the lot of you: Liz Skitch, Sharon Andrews, Lucy Best, Nicky Barry, Caili Christian, Cherie Smith, Geraldine Hickey, Lainie Chait, Eve Ellenbogen, Jo Brookfield, Jude Perl, Rachel Berger, Steph Tisdell and Abbey Newman and so many more.

To Nick Walker from Australian Scholarly Publishing who said 'A book on humour?—just what we need.' THANK YOU!

And to Eurydice Dixon: the space you should be occupying with your fabulously feisty, feminist humour remains eternally bereft.

About the Author

Justine Sless (BA, MA) is a Melbourne-based comedian, writer, humour academic and community worker. She performs, teaches, produces and writes stand-up comedy, has toured nationally and internationally, and was the former creative director of Melbourne Jewish Comedy Festival.

Justine has had short stories published in anthologies and academic journals, has written numerous one-woman shows and tailored comedy for a huge range of clients.

The COMEDY Tour is Justine's first book which began life as a Master's by Research in creative writing from La Trobe University.

www.ingramcontent.com/pod-product-compliance
Ingram Content Group Australia Pty Ltd
76 Discovery Rd, Dandenong South VIC 3175, AU
AUHW020606151225
420937AU00001B/10

9 781922 669377